WALK
WES

pocket mountains

published by

pocket mountains ltd
The Old Church, Annanside,
Moffat, Dumfries & Galloway DG10 9HB
www.pocketmountains.com

ISBN: 978-1-907025-839

Printed by J Thomson Colour Printers, Glasgow

Introduction

Lying some 50km across The Minch from the Scottish mainland at the northern end of the Outer Hebrides island chain, the Isle of Lewis – Eilean Leòdhais – is the larger, northern part of Lewis and Harris, the biggest of the Scottish islands. They are referred to as separate islands, historically because of differing clan loyalties, but also because there is a geographical 'border' of sorts, formed by the mountainous boundary of the Harris Hills and the lengthy incursions of Loch Rèasort from the west and fjord-like Loch Seaforth from the east.

North of those two sea lochs, much of southern Lewis is hillcountry and moorland, the landscape scattered with numerous freshwater lochs and lochans. Mealaisbhal in the Uig Hills in the southwest of the island is the highest peak on Lewis at 574m, while Beinn Mhòr in Pàirc in the southeast is 572m. Lewis is generally lower-lying than Harris with peat moorland covering much of the interior in the north; it also has a rugged coastline of rocky cliffs punctuated by coves, sea

lochs, small islands and skerries, and the west coast is garlanded with dune-backed white sand beaches.

History is everywhere in Lewis, with striking monuments to human endeavour – ancient and more recent – to be found in the landscape. Many of these sites – Neolithic standing stones, a Bronze Age broch, beehive cells and Victorian follies, to name but a few – are visited on the walking routes featured here.

Beyond the townships and crofting lands, the large tracts of uninhabited land around the island – coastline, mountain and moorland – are anything but empty. The landscape is dotted with poignant traces of historical settlement, cultivation and livestock management: entire townships that were cleared to make way for sheep farming, or sporting estates and communities on the periphery that were ultimately stretched too thinly. Some of these abandoned settlements are still connected by cairn-marked paths few now follow. The coast, hills and hinterland are also home to an array of magnificent wildlife.

Due to its preponderance of flatter more cultivable land, Lewis is home to three-quarters of the population of the Western Isles. Lewis and Harris are the most populous of the Scottish islands, with around 19,000 permanent residents in Lewis and 2000 in Harris. In common with Harris, Lewis remains a stronghold of the Gaelic language and of a distinctive traditional culture where the Sabbath is still widely observed.

Apart from the village of Achamore in the centre of the island, all the settlements are on or near the coast where the most fertile land is found. Crofting remains a significant part of the economic and cultural landscape of Lewis with livestock management – particularly sheep and cattle – still accounting for much crofting activity.

With a population of around 7000, Stornoway is the only town in the Western Isles and the capital of Lewis and Harris. The port town is built around a natural harbour on the eastern side of Lewis, and the ferry connects with Ullapool on the mainland. Once home to a thriving fishing industry, Stornoway now has a much reduced fishing fleet, but the town's economy has diversified over the years.

As travel to the islands has become quicker and easier, visitor numbers have increased in recent years, and tourism plays an important part in the island's economy. In the spring and summer months, the ferry port at Stornoway bustles with visitors arriving and departing in cars, campervans and motorhomes, on pannier-laden bicycles and on foot.

Lewis is very much a working place, however, with crofting, fishing and weaving still mainstays of island life. Aquaculture has become a major source of employment, and the many small enterprises add to the air of industry here. More than 40 percent of the working population is employed in the public sector, principally the local authority, Comhairle nan Eilean Siar, and the NHS.

Lewis has an abundance of walks to suit most timetables and energy levels. Although there are plenty of fine vistas and monuments a short walk from the nearest car park, some of the island's most beautiful landscapes and fascinating historical sites are accessible only on foot or by boat, which only adds to the pleasure of visiting them.

This guidebook brings together 25 of the best walking routes, from strolls along the west coast's white sand beaches and half-day outings on rugged coastal paths to day-long mountain hikes and one wild country backpacking trek.

Some of the routes are relatively popular, such as the one to the Butt of Lewis Lighthouse, the east coast Heritage Trail between Tolsta and Ness and a ramble around the grounds of Stornoway's Lews Castle.

Others are largely unfrequented, including a tour of the hills of northern Pàirc and the Àird Bheag backpacking route in southwest Lewis. Three walking options are also included for visitors to the uninhabited Shiant Islands off the east coast of Lewis.

Weather

The Hebridean weather can be challenging – high winds and persistent rain are not uncommon – but, contrary to popular myth, the sun often shines in the Outer Hebrides too. In fact, the Hebridean climate, greatly influenced by the North Atlantic Drift, is generally milder than that of the Scottish mainland. Island weather is changeable, usually providing some variety over the course of a few days, and you should be prepared and equipped for all eventualities when planning walks.

Access and safety

Public access to the countryside in Scotland is a statutory right. The Scottish Outdoor Access Code provides guidance both for those exercising their right to roam and for land managers. See outdooraccess-scotland.scot.

Walkers have the right to roam over all open land, but this also comes with responsibilities. They must treat the environment and wildlife with care, respect the needs and privacy of those living and working in the countryside, not obstruct activities such as farming, crofting and deer stalking, and keep dogs under close control near livestock and ground-nesting birds. Sheep and cattle may be encountered roaming on roads, paths and beaches, so drive aware and be alert when walking with dogs.

Check weather forecasts before setting out and allow plenty of time to complete walks. Always let someone know your intended route and estimated time of completion. While some of the routes featured here take clear paths and tracks – some signposted and waymarked, others not – others follow vague and intermittent paths at best, and require a degree of navigational competence.

Getting there and getting around

Caledonian MacBrayne ferries sail from the mainland port of Ullapool to Stornoway and from Uig, Skye to Tarbert, Harris. Book well ahead for vehicles as the ferries can be very busy, especially in summer.

Loganair flies to Stornoway from Inverness, Edinburgh and Glasgow. Lewis and Harris have a network of bus routes connecting most townships with Stornoway and Tarbert, hence many of the walks can be accessed by public transport, though timetables are often organised around schooldays.

If driving or cycling, familiarise yourself with the correct use of passing places on the island's single-track roads, including letting vehicles overtake safely.

History

There are extensive traces of Neolithic culture in the Hebrides; the best-known site is the megalithic standing stones at Callanish (Calanais) in Lewis. Bronze Age sites are also found throughout the islands, including hut circles, field systems and burial cairns.

Viking raiders arrived in the islands at the end of the eighth century and formal Norse control followed in 1098.

The Norsemen ruled the islands until 1156 when the Norse-Gael warlord Somerled took control of the Inner Hebrides. The Outer Hebrides remained in Norse hands until they were ceded to the Kingdom of Scotland at the Treaty of Perth in 1266. Somerled's descendants, Clan Donald – known as the Lords of the Isles – emerged as the most important power in northwest Scotland, ruling the isles until 1493.

With the Treaty of Union in 1707, the Hebrides became part of the new Kingdom of Great Britain, although there was considerable support for the Stuart cause among the island clan chiefs during the 1715 and 1745 Jacobite rebellions. In 1746 the decisive defeat of Charles Edward Stuart's forces at the Battle of Culloden brought serious repercussions for highlanders and islanders. The British government broke up the clan system and turned the Hebrides into a series of landed estates. The descendants of the clan chiefs became English-speaking landlords more concerned with revenues generated by their estates than the condition of those who lived on them. Rents were increased, Gaelic-speaking was discouraged and the wearing of folk dress was outlawed.

In the mid-19th century crofting communities were devastated by the Clearances. Throughout the Highlands and Islands, populations were evicted – often forcibly – and replaced with sheep and deer. In Lewis, crofting communities were uprooted from their land. Large-scale emigration followed, some voluntary, some forced, with islanders relocated to the west coast and Lowlands of mainland Scotland and the North American colonies.

The outlook for the depleted island communities remained bleak until rent strikes and land raids led to the passing of the 1886 Crofters Act. The Act set fair rents and guaranteed security of tenure and the right to bequeath crofts to a successor.

Nonetheless, emigration from the Hebrides continued apace, and many communities dwindled through much of the 20th century. For those who remained, the economic

7

situation gradually improved, with cattle farming, fisheries and tourism providing much of the stimulus. The fortunes of islanders were also influenced by the lairds, landowners and entrepreneurs who owned much of the archipelago. The philanthropic entrepreneur Lord Leverhulme invested in infrastructure and economic development on Lewis and Harris – with limited success.

The population decline affecting the Hebrides since the mid-19th century has to some extent stalled. As well as the public sector, farming, aquaculture, fishing and tourism, the development of renewable energy – wind and wave power projects – are an important element of the future island economy.

Conservation bodies and local communities have worked together in recent years to limit large-scale wind farm developments in favour of smaller community-owned projects, generating power currently consumed locally with profits ploughed back into community projects. The impetus for local control of natural assets is part of a bigger

picture for the future of the island communities. The provisions of the 2003 Scottish Land Reform Act, together with funding to support bids, has encouraged community land ownership in the Western Isles with more than three quarters of land currently in the hands of community trusts and further community buy-outs in progress.

Natural history

The Outer Hebrides are largely comprised of Lewisian gneisses, some of the oldest rocks in Europe. The rugged landscape of the present day dates from the most recent glacial period of the Quaternary ice age when much of the rocky low-lying terrain was heavily scoured by the advancing ice sheet, creating the characteristic 'cnoc-and-lochan' topography of hillocks and small lochs. Sea levels rose as the glaciers melted, resulting in the archipelago of islands, skerries and reefs recognisable today. Vast quantities of sand and gravel deposited into the sea by glacial meltwaters were swept ashore by wind and wave action, forming the white sand beaches and sand dunes characteristic of the low-lying areas of the western coastline.

There are few native mammal species in the Outer Hebrides, but the chances of spotting wildlife while out walking are good. Red deer haunt the crags and glens and are often seen when out walking, particularly in the Uig Hills and the hinterland of Pàirc. Mountain hares are generally much more difficult to see and the local population is small. They tend to be solitary and are normally found high up in the mountains. Otters have territories around much of the island's coastline and are most often to be seen around the rocky inlets and headlands of the east coast.

Common and Atlantic grey seals are abundant and are regularly spotted basking on offshore rocks and skerries or observing onshore activity from the sea. Dolphins and porpoises frequent the sea lochs and bays of the east coast, usually in the spring and summer months.

Few sights are as rewarding as a golden eagle soaring past a mountain ridge or effortlessly rising on thermals, except perhaps that of a white-tailed eagle flapping its barn door-sized wings as it patrols the coastline in search of prey. There is a good chance of spotting eagles, particularly in the hillcountry of south Lewis. Eagles aside, the birdlife of the Outer Hebrides is rich, diverse and often spectacular. A number of rare and uncommon species, native and migrant, such as the corncrake, red-necked phalarope and great northern diver are present in the islands, as are several of the most impressive and photogenic species, including the raven, gannet and puffin. See western-isles-wildlife.com for up to date information on recent sightings.

Butt of Lewis

Tolsta
Head

Arnol

Garenin

Isle of Lewis

Garynahine

Achamore

Stornoway

Baile
Ailein

Cromore

Brèinis

Uig

Pàirc

North
Harris

The Minch

Tarbert

South
Harris

Shiant
Islands

Contents

Lewis

Stornoway Harbour

Stornoway and Lews Castle

Distance 7.25km **Total ascent** 270m
Time 2 hours 30 **Terrain** pavement,
surfaced track and footpaths
Map OS Explorer 459

With a population of around 7000
the port town of Stornoway is the
capital of Lewis and Harris and
the main town of the Western Isles.
Once a thriving fishing port, the
Stornoway fleet is much reduced,
but this small coastal town still
has plenty going on these days –
though Sundays remain quiet with
most businesses closed according
to traditional religious observance.

Stornoway is compact enough to
wander around without getting lost
and there's plenty of interest around
the town and harbour area, as well
as some great restaurants, cafés,
independent shops and the award-
winning An Lanntair Arts Centre.
The obvious destination for a pleasant
walk with fine views is the grounds of
Lews Castle, immediately to the west
of the town and harbour.

The castle grounds were originally
laid out in the 1850s and have been
in community ownership since 1923.
The Grounds – as they are known
locally – have long been Stornoway's
public recreation park due to the
proximity of the town. This short walk
starts by the harbour and continues
through the castle's wooded parkland
before returning to the town.

From the North Beach car park by
the quay, where Stornoway fishing
boats moor, locate the statue of a
herring girl and exit the car park just
opposite. Turn left along Cromwell
Street, which soon swings northwards.
Continue along the street past shops,
with the marina and lifeboat station
over to the left and Lews Castle in its
parkland setting across the water, as
Cromwell Street becomes Bayhead.

Where the Bayhead River flows into
the head of the bay, turn left
(signposted Caisteal Leòdhais) just
before the Bayhead Bridge Centre and
cross a footbridge over the outflow of
the river. Turn left again to follow the
waterside track through the grounds,
which were established as part of the

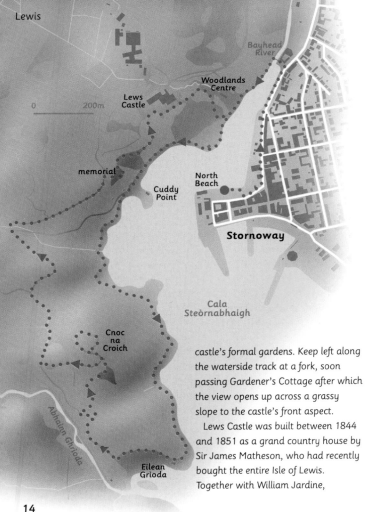

Lewis

Bayhead River

Woodlands Centre

Lews Castle

0   200m

memorial

Cuddy Point

North Beach

Stornoway

Cala Steòrnabhaigh

Cnoc na Croich

Abhainn Ghrioda

Eilean Grioda

castle's formal gardens. Keep left along the waterside track at a fork, soon passing Gardener's Cottage after which the view opens up across a grassy slope to the castle's front aspect.

Lews Castle was built between 1844 and 1851 as a grand country house by Sir James Matheson, who had recently bought the entire Isle of Lewis. Together with William Jardine,

Matheson founded the Far East trading company, Jardine Matheson & Co, making their fortune trading cotton, tea, silk and other commodities – most notably, opium. Conflict between Britain and China over attempts to expand the opium trade, lobbied for by Jardine Matheson, led to the Opium Wars of the mid-19th century.

In 1918 Lews Castle was purchased – along with the entire island – by Lord Leverhulme who set about planning for the future prosperity of the Outer Hebrides. He used his business acumen and scientific innovation to establish a thriving fishing industry while also developing various other projects.

However, some of his ambitious plans met local resistance, not least from crofters reluctant to abandon their traditional and independent way of life to fit in with Leverhulme's schemes. In 1923, having shifted his attention to neighbouring Harris, he offered the land back to the people of Lewis, but only Stornoway parish took up his offer, establishing a trust to work for the benefit of the town.

During the Second World War, Lews Castle was used to house 700 Naval Air Squadron. In the 1950s the castle was used as accommodation for students of Lews Castle College, but thereafter the building was left disused for several decades. The category A-listed building is now owned by the Comhairle nan Eilean Siar. In 2016 Lews Castle was awarded £4.6 million by the Heritage Lottery Fund to convert the site into a bilingual museum and cultural centre.

Pass the jetty and slipway at Cuddy Point, which was used for launching the six Supermarine Walrus amphibious reconnaissance aircraft based here during the last war. There are fine views across the harbour to the town.

Go through a gate and keep to the lower waterside track which weaves its way along the wooded coastline and around the headland. After some seats, follow the track around to the right to reach a T-junction. Turn right, then take the right-hand fork heading gently uphill through trees. Ignore a path on the right and follow the main track, which swings left steeply uphill. Take the next turning on the right to detour up to the hilltop of Cnoch na Croich, winding up through scrub woodland. Keep left at a fork and, where the path intersects a broader track, turn right, then fork right shortly after to reach the cairn and picnic benches at the top of the hill with Lews Castle and Stornoway spread out below. Otherwise known as Gallows Hill, this was formerly the place of execution for the Isle of Lewis. Follow the trail which loops around, then descends to rejoin the main track that you left earlier.

Bear right along this, shortly ignoring a path on the right before turning right at the T-junction a little further on. Stay with the main track, ignoring a path on the left and two on the right. Turn right at a T-junction, then after 400m head right to go down steps and through a gate to Lady Matheson's Memorial. Look out for the poppy heads adorning the pillars – an allusion to the opium trade, which contributed significantly to Jardine Matheson & Co's fortune.

Carry on from the memorial, ignoring a path descending to the right and keeping straight ahead along a path winding through the trees. This eventually emerges onto a broader path with Lews Castle now visible ahead. Head to the front of the impressive Gothic Revival-style edifice. The restored castle houses a café, function rooms, a restored ballroom and upmarket holiday accommodation. The modern addition to the castle is the museum, which houses permanent and temporary exhibitions, including six of the Lewis Chessmen on loan from the British Museum. Continue in front of the castle, along the surfaced path and straight across a bridge, then turn right alongside the road for a short way before turning right to head down past the Woodlands Centre and its café, which is well worth a visit. Turn left along the waterside track to retrace your outward route back to the start.

Lews Castle

Lewis

Coastline south of Tolsta Head

Tolsta Head and Tràigh Mhòr

Distance 11km **Total ascent** 475m
Time 3 hours 30 **Terrain** sandy
beaches, rough clifftop and moorland
terrain, waymarked path, minor roads;
boggy in places **Map** OS Explorer 460
Access bus (W5A) to New Tolsta
from Stornoway

**Some 20km to the northeast of
Stornoway, the rugged profile
of Tolsta Head (Rubha Tholastaidh)
juts eastwards into The Minch.
A walk out along this promontory
gives views across to the distinctive
mainland summits of Assynt and
along the beautiful coastline of
northeast Lewis.**

Immediately to the northwest that
coastline is fringed by the incredible
2.5km dune-backed white sand beach
of Tràigh Mhòr. This walk takes the
rough with the smooth, combining the
boggy clifftop terrain of the headland
with the vast sandy sweep of one of
the finest beaches on Lewis.

Starting from the Tràigh Mhòr
parking area beyond New Tolsta, the
route heads through the dunes behind

the beach before climbing along a
cemetery access road to North Tolsta.
Continuing southwards through the
township, the route rejoins the coast to
follow the waymarked route around
Tolsta Head before returning along the
huge expanse of beach to the start.

From the parking area, go through
the gate and follow the path across
a footbridge. Keep right and continue
along the grassy path past a picnic
table; bear right to follow a path along
the fenceline to the rear of marram
grass-covered dunes. Cross a small
burn flowing out to the beach and
climb the grassy hillock on the other
side. There are great views southeast
along the beach towards Tolsta Head
and closer to hand there is a cemetery
directly south above the dunes.
Continue southwards along the grassy
ridge and drop down to cross another
small burn. Now bear right (southwest)
to join a path passing alongside the
cemetery; head up a rise and go
through a stock gate next to the
cemetery to join the access road
heading southwestwards up through

19

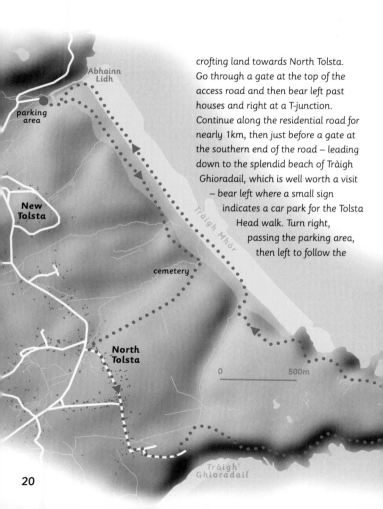

crofting land towards North Tolsta. Go through a gate at the top of the access road and then bear left past houses and right at a T-junction. Continue along the residential road for nearly 1km, then just before a gate at the southern end of the road – leading down to the splendid beach of Tràigh Ghioradail, which is well worth a visit – bear left where a small sign indicates a car park for the Tolsta Head walk. Turn right, passing the parking area, then left to follow the

parking area

New Tolsta

Abhainn Lidh

Tràigh Mhòr

cemetery

North Tolsta

0   500m

Tràigh Ghioradail

minor road towards a solitary house.

Just before you reach the crofthouse, bear left through a stock gate with a sign indicating the start of the walk. Turn right to follow the trodden path initially along the fenceline, bearing north for around 200m, then turning right along a boggy path. Look out for the first in a series of old marker posts as the path passes the last fence of the croft. The waymarked route soon reaches the clifftop beyond the enclosed croftland and there are views back along the coast to Tràigh Ghioradail and south to Tiumpan Head with its lighthouse.

Continue following the marker posts through the grass and heather-cloaked terrain along the clifftops with frequent boggy channels to cross. There are views across to the mountains on the mainland's western seaboard and down to stacks and natural arches below the cliffs. A wooden signpost

Heisgeir

Tolsta
Head

points left (north) indicating a shortcut to Heisgeir, but continue eastwards towards Rubha Tholastaidh – Tolsta Head.

Follow the marker posts around the headland where the going underfoot becomes rougher and boggier. As the route turns along the northern side of the headland there are views across to the jagged sea stacks of Heisgeir with the magnificent sweep of the Tràigh Mhòr sands beyond. Carry on contouring round to the left and at a point above the Heisgeir stacks, you'll see the counterpart of the twin signpost passed earlier. Continue northwestwards along the rough and boggy clifftops.

Go through a gate and descend along the grassy clifftop with Tràigh Mhòr beckoning below. The ground soon drops very steeply down to a burn; look for a safe route down and descend with care. Follow the burn out to the beach, turn left along the sands and continue for 2km to the Abhainn Lidh at its far end. Now head left to the car park and toilets at the start.

21

Lewis

Tolsta Head and Tràigh Mhòr

Looking north across Tràigh Mhòr

Lewis

Coastline near Cuidhsiadar

Tolsta to Port of Ness

Distance 22km **Total ascent** 650m
Time 7 hours 30 **Terrain** tracks, clifftop
paths, heathery and boggy in places
Map OS Explorer 460 **Access** bus
(W5A) to New Tolsta from Stornoway;
bus (W1) to return to Stornoway from
Lionel near Port of Ness

**A spectacular walk along the
east coast of north Lewis, the
Heritage Trail is full of historical
interest and dramatic coastal
scenery. This is a long walk; the
terrain is rough, boggy in places
and exposed to the elements –
in short, it makes for quite a
demanding excursion.**

The route described replaces the
original waymarked Heritage Trail –
still marked on OS maps – which
followed the course of an ancient
inland route through moorland.
This has now largely been subsumed
into the bog and there is little to
recommend it, whilst the new route
is comprehensively waymarked and
largely cleaves to the coast.

The distance given here is one way,

from the bus route terminus in New
Tolsta to the bus stop in Lionel. If
you're driving, there are two realistic
options: walk from the car park at
Tràigh Ghearadha and arrange a lift
from the road end at Skigersta (17km);
or walk out as far as Cuidhsiadar (the
onward track road to Skigersta is fairly
dull), then retrace your steps –
although this is a lengthy 27km.

Drivers, park at the northernmost
parking area by Tràigh Ghearadha.
If taking the bus to New Tolsta, walk to
the end of the B895, cross a cattle grid
and follow the road northwards with
views south across the sandy expanse
of Tràigh Mhòr towards Tolsta Head
and east across The Minch to the
summits of Assynt. As the road passes
around the flank of Ben Geiraha, the
beach of Tràigh Ghearadha with its
gnarly rock stacks – including Caisteal
a' Mhorair – comes into view. Continue
down to the parking area.

From here, walk northwards along
the single-track road, crossing the
'Bridge to Nowhere' over the Abhainn
Ghearadha. Other than a stretch of

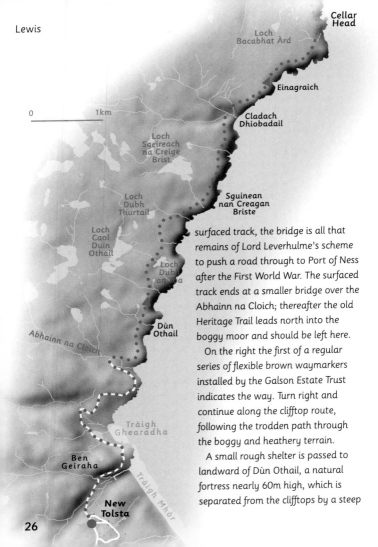

Lewis

Loch
Bacabhat Àrd

Cellar
Head

Einagraich

Cladach
Dhiobadail

0   1km

Loch
Sgeireach
na Creige
Brist

Sguinean
nan Creagan
Briste

Loch
Dubh
Thurtail

Loch
Caol
Duin
Othail

Loch
Dubh
an Fhamhair

Dùn
Othail

Abhainn na Cloich

Tràigh
Ghearadha

Ben
Geiraha

Tràigh Mhòr

New
Tolsta

surfaced track, the bridge is all that remains of Lord Leverhulme's scheme to push a road through to Port of Ness after the First World War. The surfaced track ends at a smaller bridge over the Abhainn na Cloich; thereafter the old Heritage Trail leads north into the boggy moor and should be left here.

On the right the first of a regular series of flexible brown waymarkers installed by the Galson Estate Trust indicates the way. Turn right and continue along the clifftop route, following the trodden path through the boggy and heathery terrain.

A small rough shelter is passed to landward of Dùn Othail, a natural fortress nearly 60m high, which is separated from the clifftops by a steep

26

ravine known as Nicolson's Leap. Continue northeastwards, following the trodden path and waymarker posts along the coast. Keep to landward of Loch Dubh an Toa, then continue to the east of Loch Dubh Thurtail and Loch Sgeireach na Creige Brist.

Approaching the deep cleft of Gil an Tairbh, the old path heads inland to reach the remains of the settlement at Aird Dhiobadail, going around Gil an Tairbh and Gil Dhiobadail, which merge just before flowing into the sea at Cladach Dhiobadail. The waymarked route continues straight ahead, descending steeply to cross the burn and climbing directly up the other side, although this could be tricky if the burn is in spate. Both routes rejoin near a hut and the waymarkers continue along the coast, passing the remains of stone-built shielings. There are ruined shielings at both Aird Dhiobadail and at Lower Dibadale.

Leaving Dhiobadail, follow the waymarked path along the coast, passing above an impressive landslip and soon traversing the clifftops at

Cellar Head (Rubha an t-Selieir); look out for the spectacular double natural arch below the cliffs here. Beyond Cellar Head the clifftop terrain is rough-going in places with peat hags and tussocks, and there is a fairly steep descent to cross a burn just before Filiscleitir. Once over this, cross another burn and pass stone-built ruins along the flank of the gully. The going becomes easier approaching Filiscleitir.

Traditionally, people from the township of Lionel used Filiscleitir for their summer airidhean, where cattle were moved for the summer months to benefit from fresh moorland grass and relieve pressure on the croftland. The airidhean were also popular for courting, resulting in many marriages between people from Ness and Tolsta.

The main ruin on the clifftop is Edgemoor Hall, built as a place of worship by John Nicolson. Born in Lionel, he emigrated to America where he joined the Plymouth Brethren, before returning in the 1900s with his wife and building a cliff-edge house called Dune Tower, which was

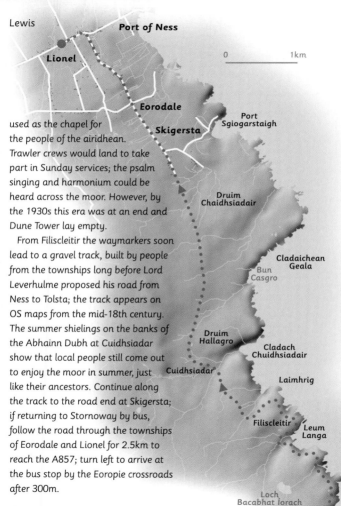

Lewis

Port of Ness

Lionel

0   1km

Eorodale

Skigersta

Port
Sgiogarstaigh

used as the chapel for
the people of the airidhean.
Trawler crews would land to take
part in Sunday services; the psalm
singing and harmonium could be
heard across the moor. However, by
the 1930s this era was at an end and
Dune Tower lay empty.

Druim
Chaidhsiadair

Cladaichean
Geala

Bun
Casgro

From Filiscleitir the waymarkers soon
lead to a gravel track, built by people
from the townships long before Lord
Leverhulme proposed his road from
Ness to Tolsta; the track appears on
OS maps from the mid-18th century.
The summer shielings on the banks of
the Abhainn Dubh at Cuidhsiadar
show that local people still come out
to enjoy the moor in summer, just
like their ancestors. Continue along
the track to the road end at Skigersta;
if returning to Stornoway by bus,
follow the road through the townships
of Eorodale and Lionel for 2.5km to
reach the A857; turn left to arrive at
the bus stop by the Eoropie crossroads
after 300m.

Druim
Hallagro

Cladach
Chuidhsiadair

Cuidhsiadar

Laimhrig

Filiscleitir

Leum
Langa

Loch
Bacabhat Iorach

28

Cellar
Head

The ruined chapel at Filiscleitir

The Butt of Lewis Lighthouse

4

Dùn Eistean and the Butt of Lewis

Distance 10km **Total ascent** 185m
Time 4 hours **Terrain** grassy clifftop
terrain, sandy beaches, rough
waymarked path, minor roads
Map OS Explorer 460
Access bus (W1) to Port of Ness
or Eoropie from Stornoway

**The northernmost corner of
Lewis is alive with small crofting
townships, bristling with historical
monuments and garlanded with
wonderful coastal scenery.**

This walking tour of the area follows
the minor road through the settlements
of Eoropie, Coig Peighinnean and
Knockaird before taking in the coastline
to the southeast and southwest of
Rubha Robhanais, the most northerly
point of the Outer Hebrides, more
widely known as the Butt of Lewis –
with its famous lighthouse. The tiny
medieval St Molveg's Church (Teampall
Mhoulaidh) and Dùn Eistean – the site
of a medieval fort atop a sea stack –
are visited on the way as are several

beautiful beaches and bays. On a fine,
calm day this route is ideal for taking
your time to appreciate the history and
splendid scenery, while a windy day
makes for a bracing experience –
especially along the exposed coastline
– and caution should be exercised.

From the parking area at Dunes Park,
head back to the B8013. Dogleg right,
then left to follow a road a short way
past houses to a T-junction with the
B8014. Turn left for 80m to find the
signed path on the right for St Molveg's
Church – which stands amid crofting
land to the rear of the village.
Curiously, the path is tightly hemmed
in by stock fences and the stone
perimeter wall is equally close-fitting.
Perhaps this is because of a need to use
all available land for grazing livestock.

At one time this diminutive church,
which dates from between the 12th
and 16th centuries, was one of three
principal centres of Christianity in the
Western Isles. During the 16th century
it was a site of pilgrimage, particularly

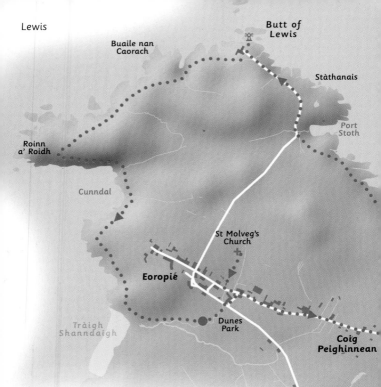

Lewis

Butt of Lewis

Buaile nan Caorach

Stàthanais

Port Stoth

Roinn a' Roidh

Cunndal

St Molveg's Church

Eoropié

Dunes Park

Tràigh Shanndaigh

Coig Peighinnean

for those seeking healing for afflictions of the body and mind. St Molveg's was restored between 1911 and 1912, and the pulpit, altar and font date from this period. There are also two tiny chapels – one either side of the main body of the church – and a Celtic cross war memorial stands near the church door

on the south side. Monthly services were reinstated in 1994 – except in the winter as dictated by the lack of heating and lighting.

Return to the road, turn back along the B8014 and continue for 2km through Eoropie to Knockaird. Head up the gravel track on the left indicated by a roadsign for Dùn Eistean (Fort) and a hand-painted sign reading 'Dùn Eisdean'. Pass the twin Bronze Age standing stones of Clach Stein on the right and a watertower to the left. Follow the track as it curves around to a gate; go through and continue with

the cairn-marked summit of Dùn Eistean visible just to the north. Cross the metal footbridge spanning the vertiginous chasm separating the sea stack from the clifftop. In springtime the cliffs are busy with nesting fulmars, and Arctic terns may be nesting here between May and August — it is an offence to disturb breeding seabirds so keep your distance.

Dùn Eistean is the site of a medieval fort, traditionally known as a stronghold of Clan Morrison — once a powerful family connected with the Lordship of the Isles dynasty. Archaeological excavations and surveying revealed the footings of several buildings, including dwellings, a barn and a grain-drying kiln. The buildings had stone and turf walls with roofs of turf or thatch. The perimeter was protected by a defensive wall and a fortified stone tower stood at the highest point of the stack. Recent finds of musket balls and pistol shot are thought to date from 1595 to 1596 when the fort was

0   500m

Dùn Eistean

Knockaird

Loch iapabhat

Port of Ness

33

besieged by a rival clan. A man-made pond for catching fresh water is still visible and archaeological evidence suggests that the site provided all that was needed for self-sufficient permanent occupation.

Head back across the bridge and continue westwards along the trodden path with occasional marker posts. Pass a sheep fank and continue along the clifftops with the corrugations of old lazy beds beneath the close-cropped turf. Follow the path past the heads of two inlets and pass through a couple of gates with the top of the Butt of Lewis Lighthouse visible as you progress westwards. The path reaches the minor road leading to the lighthouse above the sheltered sandy cove of Port Stoth, which you may feel compelled to visit. Continuing, turn right along the road and follow it around to the Butt of Lewis and its celebrated 37m-high red-brick lighthouse tower.

This northwestern tip of Lewis is exposed to the full force of the elements with Atlantic storms battering the rocky coastline and scouring the landscape. Indeed, *The Guinness Book of Records* once claimed the Butt of Lewis as the windiest place in the UK. The Butt of Lewis Lighthouse was built in 1862 by brothers David and Thomas Stevenson. They were the third generation of the famous Stevenson lighthouse-building dynasty who designed and built 97 lighthouses around Scotland's coastline and as far afield as Japan and the Strait of Malacca over the course of 126 years until 1937. Thomas' son, Robert Louis Stevenson, declined to enter the family profession, instead finding fame as a novelist and poet, authoring classics that included *Kidnapped* and *Treasure Island*. Of his family's engineering feats, he wrote: 'Whenever I smell salt water, I know I am not far from one of the works of my ancestors. The Bell Rock stands monument for my grandfather; the Skerry Vhor for my uncle Alan; and when the lights come out at sundown along the shores of Scotland, I am proud to think they burn more brightly for the genius of my father'.

Today, the lighthouse remains an important beacon for shipping while also acting as the monitoring station for the automatic lights on the Flannan Isles, North Rona and Sula Sgeir and it is the radio control station for the North Minch area. The fog signal was discontinued on 31 March 1995; the light itself was automated on 30 March 1998 and is now remotely monitored from the Northern Lighthouse Board's headquarters in Edinburgh.

To continue around the coast pass to the left of the lighthouse buildings' perimeter wall, then follow the marker posts around the grassy clifftops with views back to the lighthouse and the rugged, rocky cliffs. As you progress, the views open up to the south with the sandy beaches, dunes and croftlands of the townships dotted along the west coast. Continue around a headland, turning eastwards with views across the beaches at Cunndal

and the dunes of Tràigh Shanndaigh beyond. Go through a gate and carry on following the path along the low clifftops above Cunndal. It's possible to descend a rough slope to the beach at its southern end.

Keep on along the grassy clifftop path, soon passing through a gate with the sandy dune-backed expanse of Tràigh Shanndaigh ahead. A burn flows out across the northern side of the beach, braided channels fanning out across the sand. The path passes a stone seat and memorial stone recording the names of two fishing boat crews who were lost here during a gale in 1885. Follow the fenceline and go through a gate on the right. If venturing down to the beach, be aware of quicksands. Otherwise, bear left and continue along the fenceline, soon passing through another gate. Take the path back to the car park and children's play area at Eoropie.

Port Stoth

Looking north to Sròn Lionta
from Eilean an Taighe with the
bothy in the foreground

5

The Shiant Islands

Lying to the east of the Sound of Shiant, 7km from the Pàirc region of southeast Lewis, the Shiant Islands are an archipelago of three small islands and the Galtachan – a chain of angular sea-girt rocks.

The main islands are Garbh Eilean (Rough Island) and Eilean an Taighe (House Island), which are connected by a narrow isthmus of pebble beach with Eilean Mhuire (Mary's Island) to the east. The name 'Shiant Islands' derives from the Scottish Gaelic *Na h-Eileanan Seunta*, which approximates as the 'Holy' or 'Enchanted Isles'. The group is also known as Na h-Eileanan Mòra, 'the Big Isles'. Garbh Eilean and Eilean an Taighe have a combined area of 143 hectares while Eilean Mhuire extends to 75 hectares. Geologically, the islands are an extension of Skye's northern Trotternish peninsula. Dolerite columns – formed by the slow cooling of volcanic rocks deep underground around 60 million years ago, like those on the Inner Hebridean isle of Staffa and the Giant's Causeway on the Antrim coast – rise in towering cliffs more than 120m high on Garbh Eilean's north side.

An important colony for seabirds, the islands are home to around 60,000 breeding pairs of puffins (10 percent of the UK population) with thousands of guillemots, razorbills, fulmars and kittiwakes breeding here every year. Between 2014 and 2018, the Seabird Recovery Project eradicated the islands' population of black rats, encouraging new colonies of Manx shearwaters and storm petrels among other species. Sheep are grazed on the island by the holder of the grazing rights – currently a crofter from Scalpay.

The islands are privately owned by Tom Nicolson, son of the writer Adam Nicolson, whose memoir *Sea Room* is considered the definitive book on the archipelago. There is a simple bothy on Eilean an Taighe, where it is possible to stay by booking with the islands' owner, who can be contacted via the shiantisles.net website.

To get here, there are various boat tour and charter operators working out of Stornoway, Scalpay and Tarbert,

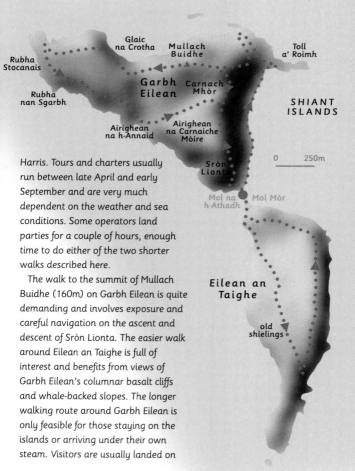

Glaic
na Crotha

Mullach
Buidhe

Toll
a' Roimh

Rubha
Stocanais

Garbh
Eilean

Carnach
Mhòr

SHIANT
ISLANDS

Rubha
nan Sgarbh

Airighean
na h-Annaid

Airighean
na Carnaiche
Mòire

Sròn
Lionta

0   250m

Mol na
h-Athadh

Mol Mòr

Eilean an
Taighe

old
shielings

Harris. Tours and charters usually
run between late April and early
September and are very much
dependent on the weather and sea
conditions. Some operators land
parties for a couple of hours, enough
time to do either of the two shorter
walks described here.

The walk to the summit of Mullach
Buidhe (160m) on Garbh Eilean is quite
demanding and involves exposure and
careful navigation on the ascent and
descent of Sròn Lionta. The easier walk
around Eilean an Taighe is full of
interest and benefits from views of
Garbh Eilean's columnar basalt cliffs
and whale-backed slopes. The longer
walking route around Garbh Eilean is
only feasible for those staying on the
islands or arriving under their own
steam. Visitors are usually landed on

Eilean Mhuire

the pebble beach of Mol Mòr between Eilean an Taighe and Garbh Eilean on the sheltered east side of the islands.

Eilean an Taighe

Distance 3km **Total ascent** 150m
Time 2 hours **Terrain** pebble beach, rough moorland terrain and clifftops, boggy in places **Map** OS Explorer 457

From Mol na h-Athadh, the pebble beach that connects Eilean an Taighe and Garbh Eilean, head SSE to climb up the rocks to a grassy path. Follow the path past some ruins and to the front of a bothy. Continue past the bothy to where the path forks. Take the left-hand fork and carry on beyond the beach, past the ruins of the head dyke with the corrugations of old lazy beds to your right. The left fork leads to a

spring, marked by a spade planted in the ground. If you need drinking water, collect it here, as there are few burns on Eilean an Taighe.

Climb uphill on the grassy track until you see the first of a number of ruined shielings. Leave the track to explore the abandoned settlement, following grassy paths connecting the ruined dwellings, with further lazy beds to the right. There are good views northwest to the rocky chain of the Galtachan lying in the Sound of Shiant.

Carry on along the track until you come to the cliff edge where you will have your first view of the fertile Eilean Mhuire, where lambs are put out to graze in spring and summer. Turn north and scramble up through the rocks onto the ridge, climbing above Eilean an Taighe's spectacular basalt cliffs to the island's summit (125m). Having enjoyed the panoramic views of the archipelago and the coast of Lewis, descend initially northwards, following the cliff edge. There are views of Eilean Mhuire to your right and of the steep rocky slopes of Garbh Eilean ahead.

41

Keep following the cliff edge as it turns northwestwards, soon crossing a boggy burn. From the headland, there are views north across the bay to the natural arch of Toll a' Roimh, otherwise known as Seal's Hole, on the eastern tip of Garbh Eilean. There are often yachts moored in the sheltered bay during summer. Continue round the headland to the finely balanced cairn perched on a rock that sits on the hill above the house. From here, you can zigzag back down the hill to the spring and follow the grassy path back past the house and Mol Mòr beyond.

Mullach Buidhe

Distance 2.5km **Total ascent** 240m
Time 2 hours **Terrain** rough hill and moorland terrain, clifftops
Map OS Explorer 457

Though it is neither a great distance nor a significant ascent, the walk to the 160m summit of Garbh Eilean is still something of a challenge – especially when undertaken within the usual time limit of a couple of hours afforded by most boat tours. The challenge comes at the beginning – and then again at the end – with the climb from the beach at Mol Mòr to the top of Sròn Lionta. It is not a route for wet or windy weather. The principal difficulty is one of finding and keeping to the safe route up – and down.

From the beach, clamber up through the rocks to join the path that zigzags uphill a short way before contouring left along the flank on steep ground. The path leads into a grassy gully, which is also steep; climb this, heading left at the top to continue up a second bump and emerge on Sròn Lionta with its commanding views back across Mol Mòr to Eilean an Taighe.

Keep heading northwards, crossing an old drystane dyke, then climbing to a cairn-marked top. Walk northwards along the ridge, passing the ruined shielings at Airighean na Carnaiche Mòire, and carry on along the clifftop at Carnach Mhòr, keeping well back from the sheer drop. The view east to Eilean Mhuire is sublime. The clifftop turns sharply westwards and a gentle climb brings you to the summit of Mullach Buidhe (160m) with views of southeast Lewis to the north and west. Retrace your outward route to return to Mol Mòr, taking care on the descent from Sròn Lionta.

Garbh Eilean

Distance 5km **Total ascent** 405m **Time** 3 hours 30 **Terrain** pebble beaches, rocky coastline, high clifftops, rough hill and moorland terrain, boggy in places; east coast only passable at low tide **Map** OS Explorer 457

The circumambulation of Garbh Eilean is high on drama, featuring towering basalt cliffs, rugged shoreline, squalls of shrieking seabirds and tremendous views from the island's whale-backed summit. Unsurprisingly, walking around 'Rough Island' isn't without its challenges. The first part of this route involves scrambling along the rocky east coast of Garbh Eilean, which is possible only at low tide. The last part of the route necessitates descending a steep gully and traversing the exposed flank of Sròn Lionta. It is not a route for wet or windy weather.

Starting from Mol Mòr at low tide only, scramble along the rocky shore fringing the bay on the island's eastern side. Ahead, the Toll a' Roimh (Seal's Hole) natural arch pierces the verdant headland framing the north side of the bay. Continue clambering over large rocks until you reach a pebble beach beneath the towering scree-skirted cliffs of Carnach Mhòr. Here thousands of puffins, razorbills and cormorants breed in spring and summer. Beyond the beach, negotiate a further short stretch of larger rocks to reach another pebble beach at the neck of the headland just west of the natural arch.

From the bay, climb a short steep grassy slope to gain the headland. It's worth visiting the promontory above the natural arch before heading northwest across old lazy beds and down to the pebble beach beneath the cliffs of Mullach Buidhe. Look out for a beautiful cup-shaped, ruined shieling above the shore. From the bay, head up the steep grassy slope at the

43

eastern end of the cliffs. Pick your way up the rock-strewn slope, which is littered with puffin burrows in the breeding season, until you gain the flatter ground atop the cliffs. Head west to the 150m summit of Mullach Buidhe, Garbh Eilean's highest point, which is not furnished with an OS trig point as the OS map suggests. From here, there are views east to Eilean Mhuire and northwest to Pàirc and the hills of Harris. Descend along the cliff edge past the ruins of the head dyke to the vertiginous cliffs at Glaic na Crotha.

Continue around the coast to Rubha Stocanais and Rubha nan Sgarbh (Cormorant Point) where the best views of the rocky Galtachan are to be had. From Rubha nan Sgarbh follow the coast to the sheep fank at Annaid, where Garbh Eilean's sheep are still gathered in for shearing each July. The ruined shielings in this grassy bay and the flowing burn make it an ideal spot for a break as there are few other places to collect water on the island.

Cross the burn and the ruined head dyke, which runs from Glaic na Crotha to Annaid, and head inland, ascending eastwards up the flank of Carnach Mhòr towards the ruined shielings at Airighean na Carnaiche Mòire, beneath which lies an Iron Age house, the largest structure ever to be built on the Shiants. From the shielings head southeast towards the cairn on the summit above Sròn Lionta.

Descend to cross a ruinous dyke at the head of two gullies, one plunging down the steep cliffs to the east and the other descending westwards to the coast. Descend southwards a little further until you reach the head of another gully descending southwestwards. Walk down through the steep grassy gully with care and after 75m or so (45m of descent) track around to your left to pick up a path that contours around the hillside above steep rocky ground (this is quite exposed) to a point above Mol Mòr. From here, it zigzags down to the pebble beach and the start.

A warming blaze in the bothy's hearth

Lewis

The Shiant Islands seen from Rhenigidale, Harris

Arnol Blackhouse Museum

6

Around Arnol

Distance 5km **Total ascent** 110m
Time 1 hour 30 **Terrain** grassy clifftop
terrain – boggy in places, minor roads
Map OS Explorer 460 **Access** West
Side Circular bus (W2) to Arnol from
Stornoway: it is quickest to travel
anti-clockwise outward and clockwise
on return

The west side crofting townships
punctuating the Atlantic-facing
coastline have much in common
with each other, though each has
its own distinctive character. Arnol's
stand-out feature is the number
of ruined blackhouses dotted
among their modern counterparts
throughout the township. These are
very substantial, well-built stone
structures with the look of great
antiquity about them, though most
were built less than 150 years ago.

The fascinating Arnol Blackhouse
Museum at No 42 is a preserved
example of the form, maintained by
Historic Environment Scotland, and is
well worth a visit before or after the
short walking tour described here.

There is a parking area just north of the
Arnol Blackhouse Museum, for use by
those visiting the historic site. There is
also limited parking (three spaces) by
the start of the waymarked route to
RSPB Loch na Muilne for those visiting
the reserve, situated to the right of the
turning circle at the road end.

Pass an RSPB interpretation panel
next to the small parking area and
head east along a surfaced track past
a house and extensive ruins on either
side. Go through a wooden gate and
look out for white-topped marker posts
leading out onto the moor. These soon
lead to a viewing area with a drystane
enclosure, stone seat and interpretation
panel overlooking Loch na Muilne and
its smaller, nearer sibling.

The rare red-necked phalaropes that
return here to breed between the end
of May and late July each year favour
the smaller loch because of the insects
found on its wetland plants. These tiny
waders subvert the usual avian gender
roles as the females have the bright
plumage while the males look after the
eggs and chicks. Other waders that can

be seen here include dunlin, redshanks and lapwings. Keep dogs on a lead and stay to the outside of the marker posts when visiting.

Follow the marker posts northwards to the coast. It's worth having a look at the steep-sided inlets and rock stacks at Geodha Mhaoir before turning southwest to continue along the coast. Several burns flow down from the loch, creating some boggy ground, so you may want to head closer to the cliff edge – with care – at this point. Climb a little to the headland of Rinn nan Gruban and look out for an impressive cairn built on the cliff edge here. Looking west, a bank of cobbles at Laingar Arnol curves out to the tide-separated Eilean Àrnol.

Keep going along the coast, soon heading down the slope towards the pebble-banked shore. Cross a fence, either by a stile or through a metal hurdle near a fence junction. Continue along the pebble bank with views south across the expanse of Loch Àrnol. The outlines of several old drystane dykes – possibly once sheep fanks – can be found on the grassy area above the pebble beach.

Head southeast to follow the surfaced track back towards Arnol, passing through the long narrow strips of crofting land radiating westwards from the township, which is largely used for grazing, but with all manner of other interesting improvised innovations going on. On reaching the T-junction with the township road, turn left and continue past houses regularly interspersed with the ruins of old blackhouses and byres. Keep left (straight on) at the junction signposted for Taigh Tughaidh Arnoil, and continue down the road for a further 600m to Arnol Blackhouse museum.

No 42 Arnol is perhaps the best-preserved example of a blackhouse on Lewis, having been transferred to state care immediately after the last occupants moved out in 1966. The thatch-roofed, stone-walled building, complete with contemporary fixtures and fittings, gives an authentic impression of living conditions in a blackhouse. At one end is a byre with stalls for housing cattle in winter, at the other is the bedroom, while the middle portion is the living room with a peat fire burning continuously in the central hearth. The peat fire is essential for keeping the roof dry and in good condition. The peat smoke also killed bugs and infused the thatch, which made excellent fertiliser for the fields when it was replaced.

The visitor centre also includes a museum and shop, the ruined blackhouse over the road at No 39 and the adjacent 'white house' built in the 1920s to replace the blackhouse.

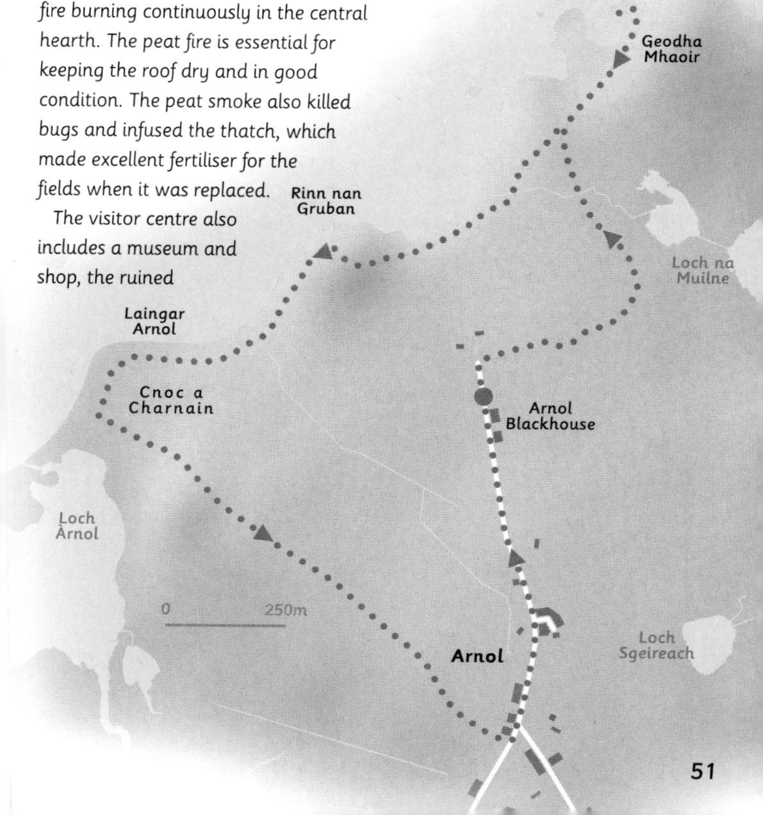

Geodha Mhaoir

Loch na Muilne

Rinn nan Gruban

Laingar Arnol

Cnoc a Charnain

Arnol Blackhouse

Loch Arnol

0   250m

Arnol

Loch Sgeireach

Looking south over
Stac a' Chaisteal

7

West Side Coastal Path

Distance 19km **Total ascent** 615m
Time 6 hours 30 **Terrain** old clifftop
paths with some boggy ground, tracks,
minor roads **Map** OS Explorer 460
Access the West Side Circular bus (W2)
from Stornoway can be used to get to
and from the start and finish. The A858
runs parallel to the coast 1km or so
inland, passing through the west side
townships at regular intervals, so the
route is never far from a road end and
can be easily cut short

**This waymarked path winds its
way across the rugged clifftop
landscape of northwest Lewis,
taking in some magnificent white
sand beaches and dramatic coastal
scenery along the way.**

The route mostly follows old paths
and the going underfoot is generally
good with some boggy sections. There
are several barbed wire stock fences to
cross, especially in the latter half of the
walk, and though crossed by stiles they
are hazardous to negotiate with dogs.
Some of the stiles towards the end
may also be in poor condition.

Walk down between the thatch-
roofed houses of Garenin Blackhouse
Village (Na Geàrrannan), pass the last
house on the right, then turn right past
an information panel and a sign for the
West Side Coastal Path and go through
a gate. Pass some ruins and continue
up along the coast, following the green-
and yellow-topped marker posts that
show the way for much of the route.
Cross a stile and climb to the highest
point on the Àird Mhòr headland,
which is marked with a small cairn.
There are grand views southwest along
the coast to Àird Laimisiadair and a
flotilla of small islands beyond. Head
eastwards, following the vague path
which stays inland from the cliff edges.
Cross the Fivig Burn near a round stone
sheep fank and keep to the marker
posts over Àird Mheadhonach.

The path soon leads past the
pinnacle-like Stac a' Chaisteal which is
joined to the cliffs by a rocky arête.
A 'blockhouse' structure was built on
the stack between 200BC and 200AD,
with defensive walls protecting its
approach from the clifftops. The path

now climbs a grassy slope between rocky outcrops, bearing inland slightly, following marker posts across boggy ground to a rocky knoll. To the northeast, the headland of Rubha an Trilleachain with its small natural arch can be seen.

The path descends across boggy ground to cross a stile near the cliffs, then heads diagonally across further boggy ground to cross another fence. Follow the path around the flank of Beinn Bheag, enjoying the views down to Bàgh Dhail Mòr, with Atlantic waves rolling ashore and a cemetery perched above the beach. Descend grassy slopes towards the landward side of the smaller cemetery, then bear right

across the burn and go through a kissing gate by the larger cemetery to reach a parking area and toilets.

Walk a short way up the road to a sharp bend. Turn left into an access road, then continue straight ahead (right) to rejoin the path initially running alongside the road. Follow the marker posts up and over the high ground between Cnoc na Moine and

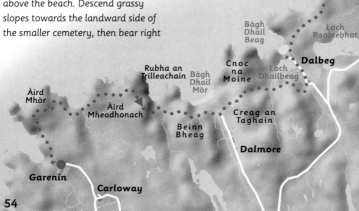

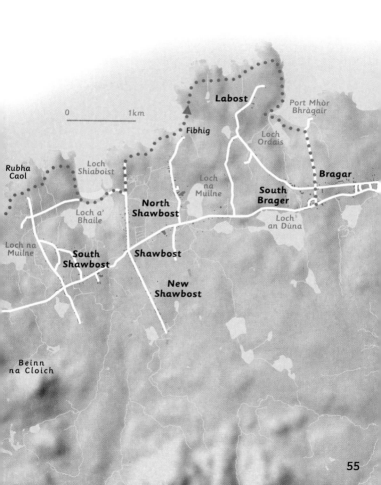

Creag an Taghain before descending towards another fence with Loch Dhailbeag below to the northeast. The path keeps to the right of the fence, climbing a little as the view opens up to Bàgh Dhail Beag. Where the fence turns sharply inland, don't continue through the gate straight ahead as this leads onto crofting land. Accompany the fence, then turn left to cross a stile. Follow the path down to a bridge over the Allt Dhail Beag, then up to the road, where you turn left and continue down towards the beach.

At the picnic area, follow the marker posts indicating the footpath on the right. Ignore the path bearing left towards the coastline and continue up the hillside to cross a stile. There are fine views back across Dalbeg with its loch, beach and rugged coastline. Carry on across easy ground, crossing fences and a drystane dyke; marker posts and stiles help to keep you on track. The coastline is stunning along this section of the route: Stac a' Phris has a large natural arch visible from the north while Rubha na Beirghe is an accessible promontory on which sits the remains of a fortified dwelling.

Just inland of Rubha Caol the route passes over a wide arch, between a deep geo (steep-sided inlet) on one side and a truly impressive blowhole on the other, which the sea funnels through at high tide. The route continues on the seaward side of fences enclosing croftland, following marker posts around Rubha Neidalt, along the western shore of Loch Shiaboist, then across the causeway separating Loch a'Bhaile from the sea.

Once across the causeway, take a minor road to a T-junction at North Shawbost. Turn left and head down to the end of the township road, passing through a gate and bearing northeast across a field to rejoin the coastline near a small bay. The route now leads you across easier ground to Fibhig, then descends to cross a raised pebble bank.

Look out for marker posts along this section as the route continues back from the sea over level, boggy ground, crossing yet more stiles and a drystane dyke. Regain the shoreline where the coastline turns south towards Port Mhòr Bhràgair. Go over a stile and take the grassy path above the shore, crossing the outflow of Loch Ordais by the shore if possible, otherwise using a wooden footbridge. Continue along a track running between the sandy bay of Port Mhòr Bhràgair and Loch Ordais before arriving at a picnic area by a minor road, which leads to a car park and cemetery. Turn right and follow the road to Bragar, keeping straight on at a crossroads in the village to reach the A858 and the bus route.

In Bragar, look out for the whalebone arch on the seaward side of the A858. In September 1920, a dead 25m-long blue whale drifted into a bay known locally as Geodha nam Muc with the harpoon that had killed it still protruding from its back. The whale became jammed in an inaccessible position, but local men in two small boats managed to tow the carcass around to Bragar Bay. A great deal of oil was recovered from the whale, but much of the decaying carcass proved unusable. However, the village postmaster and general merchant, Murdo Morrison, decided that the whale's jawbone would make a fine archway over the gate to his house at Lakefield. The following autumn the bones of the lower jaw were recovered from the whale's skeleton and hauled up from Bragar Bay. Steel plates were used to join the bones at the top with a decorative finial placed at the apex and the fatal harpoon suspended between the jawbones. Measuring around 7.5m each and weighing about four tonnes, the bones were recently restored and coated with protective fibreglass to prevent further decay. The arch stands at around 6m from ground to apex.

Stac a' Phris natural arch near South Shawbost

Heading east from the
abandoned township
of Caimishader

8

Garenin and Àird Laimisiadair

Distance 8.5km **Total ascent** 310m
Time 3 hours **Terrain** rocky, peaty
clifftop terrain, boggy in places
Map OS Explorer 460 **Access** West Side
Circular Clockwise bus (W2A) to
Garenin Village from Stornoway

**At the southwestern extremity of
northwest Lewis, the rugged Àird
Laimisiadair peninsula stretches
westwards into the Atlantic at the
mouth of Loch Ròg an Ear.**

Starting from the restored blackhouse
village at Garenin (Na Geàrrannan) on
the northwest coast, this stimulating
walk heads southwest to the tip of the
peninsula with its dramatic coastal
landscapes and views westwards to
Great Bernera and the islands of Loch
Ròg. Returning along the peninsula's
south coast the route continues through
the poignant ruins of the abandoned
crofting settlement of Laimishader –
one of the first to be cleared at the end
of the 18th century. The rough
intermittent coastal paths give way to
tarmac as a single-track road leads
through the crofting township of

Borrowston and back to Garenin.

The Garenin Blackhouse Village is
found at the end of the Garenin road
and it sits just above the village bay.
From the car park, walk down through
the thatched houses of Garenin. This
was the last inhabited settlement of
blackhouses in the Western Isles. The
last elderly residents moved to nearby
council housing in 1974 and the
abandoned blackhouses soon fell into
disrepair. In 1989 the Garenin Trust
(Urras nan Geàrrannan) was
established by the Western Isles Council
to restore the houses. Traditional
building methods were used to restore
the stonework and thatched roofing of
the houses while modern facilities were
incorporated internally. The project
was completed in 2001 and the
restored village was opened in June
that year by Princess Anne. Today,
there is a museum (a blackhouse set in
the 1950s), a resource centre, a café
and a small gift shop, which are open
in the summer months. There is also a
hostel and four self-catering cottages
among the renovated houses.

The term *tigh dubh*, or 'blackhouse', originated in the mid-19th century to distinguish this older style of house – with double thickness stone walls and thatched roofs – from the *tigh geal* or 'white house' design with single-thickness stone walls pointed with lime mortar, which came into use in the latter half of the 19th century. Although the blackhouses look quite basic they were cleverly designed, making use of the locally available materials. The insulating properties of the thatch, the double-thickness stone walls, the low profile and the rounded corners of the outside walls, which reduce the impact of the wind, all protect against the worst of the Hebridean weather.

Pass the sign for the West Side Coastal Path and continue through the gate, following the track down to the pebble bank above the shore. Bear left across the pebbles, then head up to the fence and go through the gate on the left.

There are stretches of trodden path

along the coastline – route-finding isn't difficult, but the peaty soil can be boggy in places. Bear right to follow the coast around the low-lying headland of Rubha nan Gearrannan, making for the cairn on the high point; there are great views southwest to Craigeam, an islet sitting just off Àird Laimisiadair with its

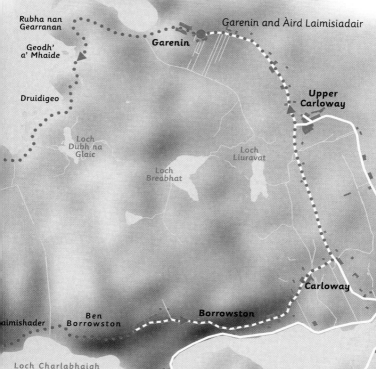

Garenin and Àird Laimisiadair

Rubha nan Gearranan

Geodh' a' Mhaide

Druidigeo

Loch Dubh na Glaic

Garenin

Upper Carloway

Loch Liuravat

Loch Breabhat

Carloway

Laimishader

Ben Borrowston

Borrowston

Loch Charlabhaigh

small modern lighthouse beacon clearly visible. Head south with the coastline towards the next inlet at Geodh' a' Mhaide. Pass to the rear of the inlet and bear right to cross a stile over a fence. Continue by the rocky coastline at Druidigeo, soon passing through a dilapidated drystane dyke, then

heading through a gap in another wall either side of a stony beach.

A short distance further on, pass an old stone sheep pen by the shore — likely once used for dipping sheep. Carry on up to the cairn atop Rubha Talanish, a fine vantage point for views back along the coast. Head south a short way, then continue across the corrugations of old lazy beds and a bank of large pebbles between the sea and freshwater Loch Rinn na Geodha.

Climb up and across the adjacent headland and descend with care away from the cliff edge at the next inlet. Walk across old lazy beds inland from the headland at A' Bheirigh, then follow the easier slopes up towards cairn-topped Meall Mòr.

Bear right to the lighthouse atop Àird Laimisiadair – a small modern beacon with a square metal tower. The higher ground here has commanding views southwest over Loch Ròg an Ear to the island of Great Bernera and west to the islands of Little Bernera, Campaigh, Cealasaigh, Sean Bheinn and Beireasaigh.

Head southwards along the ridge to the cairn and continue along the coast, crossing wet ground between Loch na h-Airde and the sea, following the vague paths where you can. The broch

of Dùn Carloway can be seen across Carloway Loch.

Look out for a trodden path following the coastline and take this across the southern flank of Ben Laimishader to reach the ruins at Laimishader, which in 1796 became one of the first townships on Lewis to be cleared. Continue past the ruins above the bay of Port Laimishader and make for a gap in the drystane dyke to pick up the remarkable old path between Laimishader and Borrowston. The stone-paved path bears right, then zigzags up above the cliffs – there are good views back across Laimishader. The gradient eases as the path continues below the flank of Ben Borrowston. Go through a stock gate to reach the surfaced road leading through the crofts at Borrowston. Continue along the road to a T-junction and turn left along the road, keeping left (straight ahead) at the next junction to return to Garenin.

Rugged coastline west of Garenin

9

Dùn Carloway

Distance 5.75km **Total ascent** 115m
Time 2 hours 30 **Terrain** rough
moorland terrain, unwaymarked path,
minor roads; boggy in places
Map OS Explorer 460 **Access** West
Side Circular Clockwise bus (W2A) to
Dùn Carloway from Stornoway

**Like the standing stones just along
the road at Callanish (Calanais),
the imposing 2000-year-old ruin of
Dùn Carloway Broch is a must-see
for visitors to Lewis.**

The sites' proximity means that many
people visit both of these marvellous
ancient monuments together. There is a
dedicated waymarked route – the
Bonnet Laird Walk – that links the two
sites, though at 15km and featuring a
fair amount of boggy ground it won't
be for everyone. The route described
here is a more modest walk taking in a
loop of moorland immediately to the
south of Dùn Carloway. The walk
follows the course of an ancient path
past lochs and peat cuttings to reach
the Doune Braes Hotel by the A858,
before returning to Dùn Carloway

Dùn Carloway Broch

Lewis

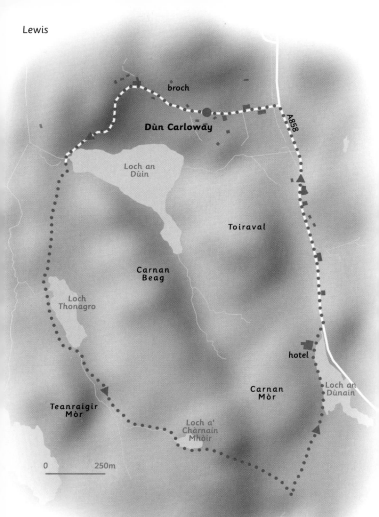

broch

Dùn Carloway

A858

Loch an Dùin

Toiraval

Carnan Beag

Loch Thonagro

Teanraigir Mòr

Carnan Mòr

hotel

Loch an Dùnain

Loch a' Chàrnain Mhòir

0   250m

alongside the road. It is probable that this path was used by children walking to and from the old local school, which latterly became the hotel. The walk starts from the parking area near the broch, which can either be visited before or after your walk.

The best-preserved broch in the Outer Hebrides, Dùn Carloway was likely built at some point between 200BC and 100AD and remains an impressive structure some 2000 years later. The external wall stands over 9m high, but would have originally been higher. The double-walled structure also had a wooden floor 2m above ground level and there may have been another floor above this. The ground floor would have been for animals, with living spaces on the upper floors accessed via stairs climbing between the inner and outer walls.

Standing on a rocky outcrop looking northwards to Loch Chàrlabhaigh, the broch is thought to have been a defensive refuge that could accommodate an extended family and their livestock in case of attack.

It appears to have been largely intact until 1601 when the Morrisons of Ness used it as a stronghold to defend themselves against the MacAulays of Uig whose cattle they had stolen. Donald Cam MacAulay scaled the outer wall and threw in burning heather, asphyxiating the Morrisons. The MacAulays then set about destroying the broch. The ruin was further dilapidated by the removal of stones for building blackhouses nearby. The removal of much of the stone on the north side has created a cut-away section through the walls, which gives a clear picture of how the broch was constructed.

In 1882 Dùn Carloway became one of the first protected ancient monuments in Scotland; it was taken into state management in 1887 and is now looked after by Historic Environment Scotland.

From the parking area, turn right to head west along the road through the crofting township of Dùn Carloway and carry on downhill to the road end by the westernmost tip of Loch an Dùin,

Lewis

Stairway between the walls
of Dùn Carloway Broch

crossing a small stone slap and pillar bridge. Continue straight ahead, ignoring the gated track on the right, and go through a stock gate. Follow the indistinct path through often boggy terrain using the intermittent stepping stones that indicate this was once a well-established path, likely used by children as the route to school at Doune Braes. Keep to the left of the fence when approaching Loch Thonagro. Bear right to skirt around the western side of the loch, climbing to higher ground. Ignore a gate, keep left of the fence and step over a burn using the two small strategically-placed boulders, which further indicate that this was once a well-used route. Cross the rough ground above the loch, descend through a gate and make for the head of the loch.

After crossing the narrow burn flowing into the loch, follow its east side southeastwards up a wide glen. If the ground is boggy, bear left to the east side of the glen where drier ground and sheep tracks aid progress. Continue gently uphill, shadowing the burn southeastwards past old peat cuttings. Follow the grassy breaks in the dense heather cover and make your way between the rocky outcrops to reach the outflow of Loch a' Chàrnain Mhòir.

Looking west there are views across Loch Ròg to Great Bernera and a flotilla of smaller islands. Bear right to follow sheep trods around the south side of the loch to its eastern end and continue past old peat cuttings, descending eastwards to join a track, which is visible ahead by a line of telegraph poles. Turn left along the track, passing more recent peat cuttings. In the opposite direction, the track leads to Tolsta Chaolais and was once used by children walking to and from the school, which is now the Doune Braes Hotel.

Pass Loch an Dùnain, go through a gate and continue past the hotel. Turn left and continue on the verge alongside the A858 for 1km, passing opposite houses before taking the first turning on the left to return to the Dùn Carloway Visitor Centre.

Iron Age house at Bostadh

Great Bernera and Bostadh

Distance 11.5km **Total ascent** 290m
Time 4 hours **Terrain** minor roads,
moorland; the waymarked route has
some pathless sections, which can be
boggy in places **Map** OS Explorer 458
Access bus (W3) to Breaclete, Bernera
from Stornoway

**The island of Great Bernera – or
Bernera as it's commonly known –
juts north into Loch Ròg an Ear
from the 'mainland' of northwest
Lewis. The 8km long by 5km wide
island has five townships: Hacklete,
Kirkibost, Tobson, Croir and
Breaclete – where both churches,
school, post office, shop and
community centre are located.**

There are currently around 300
islanders, half the number recorded in
the 1899 census. Enforced emigration
and economic hardship both played
their parts in population decline – a
trend arrested in part by the building of
the roadbridge connecting the island
with Lewis in 1953. Despite the road
link, Bernera retains a distinctive island
character of its own.

In 1962 Great Bernera, along with
the islands of Little Bernera and Eilean
Chearstaidh, were bought by the
Scottish aristocrat, Count Robin de la
Lanne Mirrlees who, despite owning a
castle and various other homes, chose
to live in a crofthouse on the island
until his death in 2012. A former
soldier and well-known ladies' man,
he was perhaps best known for
inspiring the James Bond character
through his correspondence with the
author, Ian Fleming, while he was
researching his novel, *On Her Majesty's
Secret Service*. The secret agent's
cover as genealogist Sir Hilary Bray
was based on the Count's previous role
as a heraldic researcher at the College
of Arms in London. By all accounts,
Count Robin – as he was known locally
– was immensely well liked on Great
Bernera; he supported many local
causes and readily released land for
community use.

This waymarked route loops around
the northern half of the island, starting
from Breaclete. The route follows the
road to Valasay, crosses the footbridge

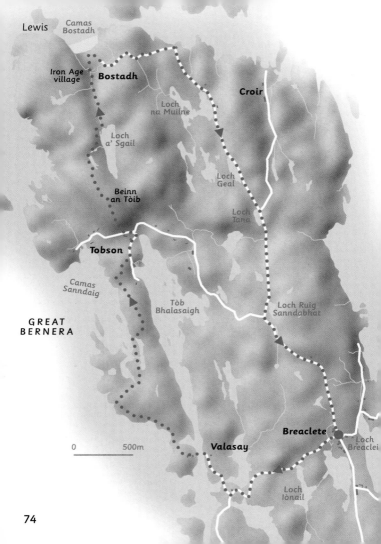

Lewis

Camas
Bostadh

Iron Age
village

Bostadh

Loch
na Muilne

Croir

Loch
a' Sgail

Loch
Geal

Loch
Tana

**Beinn
an Tòib**

Tobson

Camas
Sanndaig

Tòb
Bhalasaigh

Loch Ruig
Sanndabhat

**GREAT
BERNERA**

0   500m

Valasay

Breaclete

Loch
Breaclei

Loch
Iònail

74

over Tòb Bhalasaigh, joins a waymarked footpath heading north along the coast to the township of Tobson, then climbs over Beinn an Toib before descending to the reconstructed Iron Age house at Bostadh on the north coast, with its magnificent beach and views. There are also public toilets at Bostadh. The route then continues along the minor road, soon heading south back to the start at Breaclete.

From the community centre, turn right, heading west along the road towards Hacklete. Turn right at the junction and continue through the township of Valasay to the road end and cross the footbridge spanning the neck of Tòb Bhalasaigh. The sheltered freshwater-fed tidal lagoon is a designated Site of Special Scientific Interest because of the rare seaweeds found only in the unusual mixed freshwater and saltwater environment. The footbridge was built in 1898 to serve islanders on the coastal side of the lagoon. Turn right past the first cottage and right again as you approach the second house, through three gates. To the west are fantastic views of Tràigh na Beirigh at Reef.

Follow the waymarkers north along the west coast and, as you approach Camas Sanndaig, look out for the remains of a stone lobster pond if the tide is low. On reaching a track road follow it north to Tobson, thought to be the oldest township on Great Bernera. Bear left at the junction and after 150m turn right to follow the waymarkers gently up the ridge to the summit of Beinn an Tòib. To the west lie the islands of Pabaigh Mòr and Bhacasaigh with the sweep of white sand at Tràigh na Beirigh beyond.

Continue past Carnan Gibegeo and go through a gate in a drystane dyke. Head down the path through the small glen, following the burn flowing north from Loch a' Sgail to reach the deserted village of Bostadh beside its splendid beach.

The formerly thatched, now turf-roofed structure above the beach is a reconstruction of a house from the late Iron Age village which was discovered here in 1993 when a severe storm cut away the dunes to expose a series of stone structures. The archaeology department of the University of Edinburgh excavated the site in 1996 and found evidence of a Norse settlement. Beneath this, a series of five remarkably well-preserved Pictish 'figure of eight' houses up to 1500 years old were discovered. The excavations revealed a series of connected stone-walled houses without windows or chimneys. Each house had a long low entrance passage leading to a large circular room with an open hearth in the centre and one or more rooms opening off it. The floors were below ground level with the entrances at the southern end to keep the wind out as far as possible.

The excavations also provided extensive evidence of the inhabitants' daily lives – unsurprisingly they fished, hunted deer and seabirds, grew crops and kept livestock. Other finds showed that they also practised various crafts and kept spiritual observances. The reconstructed house, which is sadly no longer open to the public, is in an area free of actual archaeological remains; the excavated houses were reburied for preservation. There are ruined blackhouses throughout the glen, built from the Middle Ages onwards. Bostadh remained occupied until 1878 when the village was finally abandoned as the last of the peat used for fuel was exhausted. Although some of the Bostadh families emigrated to Canada, most moved to nearby Kirkibost.

To the eastern side of the bay, perched on a seaweed-covered rock, the curious object supported by a tripod is a Time and Tide Bell, created by British sculptor Marcus Vergette and Australian bell designer Neil McLachlan, which was installed at Bostadh in 2010. This is one of a number of Time and Tide Bells installed round the coast of Great Britain. Each bell is set ringing by the rising waters around high tide; the pattern of their ringing will change as sea levels rise due to climate change.

From the cemetery at Bostadh, follow the road initially eastwards. From the top of the rise, there are views along the west coast and on a clear day you can see the Flannan Isles 40km to the west. At the bottom of the hill, the road turns sharply southwards: continue for 2.5km to the Tobson junction and keep left (straight ahead) towards Breaclete.

At the junction, you will see a cairn and plaque which was erected in 1992 'To Commemorate the Participants in the Bernera Riot of 1874', when a group of crofters made a stand against the tyrannical behaviour of the landlord and his factor. In 1872 the landowner reduced the islanders' summer grazings on mainland Lewis in order to use the land for a sporting estate. Initially the crofters offered no resistance, but when the factor issued a notice sequestering the remaining grazings the islanders made a stand. The factor dispatched the Sheriff Officer to Bernera with eviction orders for 58 families; however, on arrival in Tobson the bailiffs were pelted with clods of earth. Three men were arrested and charged, but following an inspired defence in court they were acquitted in what was the first documented victory for Highland crofters against oppressive landowners.

The Bernera court case is seen as the beginning of the crofters' fight-back, which eventually led to the Napier Commission and land reform for the Highlands and Islands. Continue along the road to return to the start.

Dunes cast a shadow on
Tràigh na Beirigh, Reef

Reef

Distance 4.5km **Total ascent** 105m
Time 2 hours **Terrain** sandy beach,
dunes, rough and rocky high ground
with some slightly boggy areas
Map OS Explorer 458 **Access** bus (W4)
to Tràigh na Beirigh from Stornoway

**Projecting eastwards from the
northernmost headland of West
Uig, the Bhaltos peninsula is
surrounded on three sides by the
sea and a coterie of islands while
inland it is demarcated by the
steep-sided glen running between
Loch Miabhaig in the south and
Camas na Clibhe in the north.**

There are five villages dotted around
the peninsula: Cliff (Cliobh) sits
towards the north end of the glen,
Valtos (Bhaltos) is the largest township
at the north of the peninsula with its
neighbour Kneep (Cnip) to its south.
Reef (Riof) is at the southeast and
Uigen (Uigean) at the southern tip.

The peninsula has a long history of
settlement and the landscape is full of
traces from the Bronze Age, Iron Age
and the Norse occupation, including

brochs, wheelhouses, farmsteads and
burial grounds. The peninsula is also
fringed with beautiful beaches,
including the long white strand of
Tràigh na Beirigh at Reef. The beach is
backed by a rugged, rocky hinterland
while across the narrow sound lie the
islands of Siaram Mòr, Bhàcsaigh and
Pabaigh Mòr, further enhancing the
peninsula's great natural beauty.

Plenty of people, islanders and
visitors alike, come here to wander up
and down the beach with or without
children and dogs. In summer, it can be
relatively busy, especially as there are
site facilities for motorhomes,
campervans and tents here – even in
winter you'll be lucky to have the
beach to yourself, though there's
plenty of it to go around. This short
route does what everyone else does –
walks up and down the beach – but it
also visits the high ground to the rear
of the eastern end of the beach, scaling
the vertiginous 86m summit of Beinn
na Bheirigh and visiting a secluded
beach looking south onto Loch Ròg.

From the car park, go through a gate

Cliff

Loch
Triallabhat

by the toilets and campsite facilities
and continue through the dunes.
Pass through another gate and drop,
literally, down to the beach – you may
have to hop across a water-filled
channel beneath the dunes. Turn right
and head along the white sand strand,
which terminates abruptly at the
wedge-shaped headland of Stung more
than 1km to the east. Carry on along
the beach, soon reaching the outflow
of Loch na Bheirigh where it runs out
through a shifting shallow channel
across the sands. Hop your way across
wherever it is easiest.

Now head up through the dunes and
make for a gate at a right angle in the
stock fence at the foot of Beinn na
Bheirigh's north ridge. Go through the
gate and follow a vague path beneath
the nose of the ridge. Cross a small
burn flowing out of a narrow gorge
and climb the path on the opposite
side, soon bearing right to head south.

On reaching Loch a' Pheallair,
cross its outflow and continue
southwestwards up towards the
unmarked summit of Beinn na Bheirigh
(86m). Although the hill is of modest
height, the views are quite
outstanding, especially north across
Tràigh na Beirigh and Caolas Phabaigh
to the islands in the bay – Siaram Mòr,
Bhàcsaigh and Pabaigh Mòr.

Continue southwards down the ridge
a short way, then swing left and drop
down to cross a slightly boggy
declivity, making for the fish-tailed end
of a small lochan. Skirt around the tail
of the lochan and then turn right to
head down another damp declivity
towards Loch Lionais below. Just before
you reach the outflow of the loch, bear
left across the rocky foot of Tairaval
and then contour on vague paths
around to a fine little sandy beach
looking southeastwards across island-
dotted Loch Ròg. This is a great

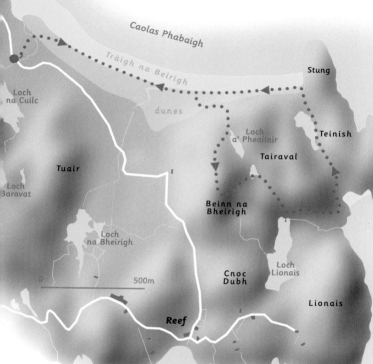

Caolas Phabaigh

Tràigh na Beirigh

Stung

Loch
na Cuilc

dunes

Teinish

Loch
a' Pheallair

Tairaval

Tuair

Loch
Baravat

Beinn na
Bheirigh

Loch
na Bheirigh

500m

Cnoc
Dubh

Loch
Lionais

Reef

Lionais

sheltered spot for a dip or a picnic.

Leaving the beach behind, head northwest up the little glen, keeping to the right-hand side as you progress and soon following a path alongside Teinish. The path crosses the edge of the dunes beneath the rocky flank of Stung; where the stock fence doesn't quite meet the rockface, squeeze through and drop down to Tràigh na Beirigh once again. Continue back along the beach, enjoying the white sands, turquoise waters and exquisite views as you go.

Looking over Dun Borranais to Ardroil

Uig Sands

Distance 3.5km **Total ascent** 35m
Time 2 hours **Terrain** track, path,
sandy beach and dunes; accessible at
lower tides only **Map** OS Explorer 458
Access bus (W4) to the Ardroil Beach
turning from Stornoway

**The vast Tràigh Ùige, or Uig Sands,
is one of the most spectacular
beaches in all of the Western Isles
archipelago. The sheer expanse
of its white sands is impressive
enough, but it is the setting with
the lunar Uig Hills as a backdrop
which makes this such a remarkable
stretch of coastal landscape.**

The area is also full of geological and
historical interest so while this walk
isn't particularly long, there's plenty to
detain you. Please note that the walk is
not possible while the tide is right in.
Do not attempt to cross back over the
sands from the Timsgarry side if the
tide is coming in.

The sands lie to the west of the
glacial meltwater channel of Gleann
Bhaltois, a narrow gorge some 2.5km
long and 45m deep at its maximum,

which was carved out of the bedrock
by meltwaters carrying heavy loads
of pebbles and cobbles. Glacial
meltwaters also swept huge quantities
of sand and gravel into the sea,
spreading the debris over much of what
is now the continental shelf. As the sea
level rose, an admixture of glacial
sediment and the tiny fragments of
crushed mollusc shells was swept
ashore by wind and wave action,
forming the white sand beaches and
sand dunes characteristic of the low-
lying areas of the western coastline.

Head down the track road signposted
for Tràigh Eader Dha Fhadhail/Ardroil
Beach and continue to the parking
area by the public toilets and campsite
facilities. Follow the track past the
parking for campervans and
motorhomes and, on reaching the
parking area at the end of the track,
turn left and head north across the
expanse of white sand. Make for the
western (left) side of the promontory
jutting southwards into the sands. The
outflow of Lòn Erista flows along this
side of the promontory, but as you

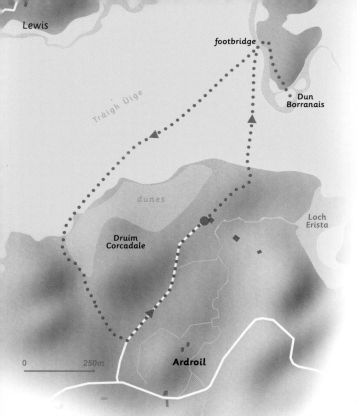

footbridge

Dun
Borranais

Tràigh Ùige

dunes

Loch
Erista

Druim
Corcadale

0   250m

Ardroil

approach a footbridge over the river
becomes apparent.

There are stepping stones leading to
the bridge, which are often slippery.
These may even be buried under the
sand by tidal displacement. Cross the

bridge, climb the slope and bear right
along the trodden path heading south
along the promontory. The path climbs
a little to the right of prominent old
lazy bed ridges, then drops down to
the southern tip of the promontory.

Here lies a tiny tidal island upon which sits the dilapidated remains of Dun Borranais, a small Iron Age fort. The site is also known as Dun Cuithach after a mythological giant who terrorised the area until he was killed by the Fians. The outer wall of the structure measures approximately 15m by 13m and is still clearly visible. The interior was later modified by the construction of two bothies against the north and south walls. The island is connected by a causeway formed of large stones – even when the tide is out water might sit in the channels around the promontory. Return along the path and recross the bridge.

Head back across the sands, bearing southwest towards the dunes, and after 1km take a path up through the dunes between two rocky hillocks. Pass to the left of the walled burial ground and cross a stile into a fenced enclosure containing a large wooden sculpture of one of the Lewis Chessmen and an information panel.

Mostly carved from walrus ivory and dating from the 12th century, a collection of 78 chess pieces formed the greater part of a hoard found in the dunes near here in 1831 by one Malcolm 'Sprot' Macleod. It is thought the pieces were made in Trondheim, which was the medieval capital of Norway. The Outer Hebrides were under Norse rule at the time. Today, the majority of the pieces are owned and usually exhibited by the British Museum in London, 11 are at the National Museum of Scotland in Edinburgh and six pieces are now on permanent display at the Lews Castle museum in Stornoway.

Turn left along the road to return to the parking area or right to continue to the Ardroil turning for the bus.

Lewis

Cliffs at Lèirigeo

13

Àird Mhòr Mhangarstaidh

Distance 4.5km **Total ascent** 215m
Time 2 hours **Terrain** sandy beach,
exposed clifftops, boggy ground,
tracks and minor road
Map OS Explorer 458 **Access** bus (W4)
to Mangersta Turn from Stornoway; or
ask to be let down at the path down to
Tràigh Mhangarstaidh

**The coastal landscape by the
small crofting township of
Mangersta is rocky, rugged and
exceptionally beautiful. The views
from the clifftops are often
exhilaratingly dramatic, especially
when the wind-driven Atlantic
batters the coastline — as it
frequently does.**

This walk visits Mangersta's beach
and cliffs before returning through the
township. As well as fabulous views,
the clifftop landscape is full of historical
and geological interest. A more recent
feature in a spectacular location is also
visited along the way. The clifftops are
exposed to the elements and the cliff
edges are undercut in places so exercise
caution. There are working crofts all

around Mangersta, so please close all
gates and be aware of livestock.

Around 1.3km along the road west
of the turning for Mangersta, there is
a small parking area in an old quarry
near a sign indicating a track down to
the shore (NB012307). Follow the path
down to the Atlantic-facing beach at
Tràigh Mhangarstaidh, its sandy
expanse framed by rugged Lewisian
gneiss cliffs and rocky outcrops. When
you're able to tear yourself away, cross
the dunes on the north side of the
beach, follow a vague path leading up
the grassy slope and make for the
prominent cairn on the clifftop. There
are fine views back across the bay to
Mealaisbhal and the Uig Hills. Continue
northwards with care along the
clifftops, enjoying the tremendous
views across the coastal landscape of
promontories, cliffs and sea stacks.

Pass high above a small bay, taking
care near the cliff edge, then follow a
path next to a grassy slope with the
corrugations of old lazy beds on the
right. It's possible to head left down to
the T-shaped promontory for some

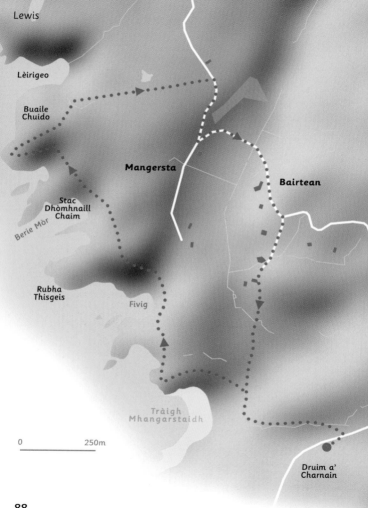

Lewis

Lèirigeo

Buaile
Chuido

Mangersta

Bairtean

Stac
Dhòmhnaill
Chaim

Berie Mòr

Rubha
Thisgeis

Fivig

Tràigh
Mhangarstaidh

0   250m

Druim a'
Charnain

great views, but do so with care.

Continue along the clifftop above the next bay and, at its far corner, cross an old stile over a stock fence – to the right a stock gate leads to a track road. Stay inland of the clifftop fence as you proceed – the rocky fin of Stac Dhòmhnaill Chaim soon appears, jutting from the cliffs. Translating from Gaelic as 'one-eyed Donald's stack', the fortified promontory was, according to tradition, the refuge of early-17th century Uig hero, Donald Cam Macaulay who was a chieftain of the Macaulays of Lewis.

The stack holds the remains of a cottage, a sheep pen and a defensive wall on the landward side; it was previously accessible via a narrow rocky isthmus with a steep drop either side, though coastal erosion has rendered it inaccessible except to climbers. Ongoing erosion and winter storms will likely destroy the site, which is a scheduled monument, in the coming decades.

Another 500m or so further on, you reach a rocky area of exposed Lewisian gneiss on the clifftop south of Lèirigeo. Here, tucked in against a rocky outcrop at the top of a sheer cliff face, is the most remarkably conceived and impressively located bothy in all of Scotland. Designed in the style of the ancient monastic beehive cells dotted around the Hebrides, the bothy was built more than 30 years ago by local crofters, John and Lorna Norgrove.

Over the years a slow trickle of people made the pilgrimage to stay at the tiny timber-framed and stone-walled structure, but in the last few years it has become popular to the point that overnight stays need to be booked a long way in advance. Even so, just visiting to admire the bothy in its unusual setting makes for a very worthwhile excursion.

The bothy also serves as a memorial to the Norgroves' daughter Linda, an aid and development worker who was kidnapped in Afghanistan in 2010 and died during an attempted rescue by US Forces. Linda was a highly qualified and dedicated environmental expert who had worked in Afghanistan since 2005, initially as an environmental and rural development officer for the UN. In Linda's memory and to continue her work, John and Lorna established the Linda Norgrove Foundation in October 2010, a trust that funds education, health and childcare for women and children in Afghanistan.*

Unless returning by your outward route, continue north a short way and cross a stock fence via a stile to arrive above the dramatic, steep-sided inlet of Lèirigeo with its gneiss cliffs and huge broken blocks of tumbled rock. Head east – inland – across open ground, weaving a course between peat hags and pools to arrive at an access road in the vicinity of a large agricultural shed. Turn right and continue through a stock gate across

the road at the northern end of Mangersta. Walk down the road to a junction – look out for the idiosyncratic 'water feature' on the right – and then turn left, or 'That Way' according to the rather unique signpost.

Carry on along the road, passing a couple of houses and a red phonebox. The road climbs and then, just past the Mangurstadh Gallery with its camping pods and huts, turn right onto a tarmac lane and follow this down towards some houses. Keep left as the road becomes a track, go through a gate and continue down towards the sandy slope to the rear of Tràigh Mhangarstaidh. Where the track bends to the right follow a path to the left and cross the burn to reach the sands. Continue down to the beach and retrace your outward route.

* To learn more about the work of the Linda Norgrove Foundation, visit **lindanorgrovefoundation.org**

The clifftop bothy at Mangersta

Looking northwest to Tràigh Uige
from Suaineabhal's summit cairn

14

Suaineabhal

Distance 14km **Total ascent** 610m
Time 6 hours **Terrain** rough, rocky
mountain and moorland terrain, a little
boggy in places **Map** OS Explorer 458
Access bus (W4) from Stornoway; ask
to be let down at Uig waterworks
turning, 1.5km from the start

**Overlooking the vast expanse of
Tràigh Ùige, Suaineabhal is the
most prominent outlier of the main
group of the Uig Hills ranged on
either side of Gleann Raonasgail
and Gleann Tamnasdail. At 428m,
it is not as lofty as its near
neighbours, but what it lacks in
height it makes up for in stature
and the views afforded by its
isolated position.**

There are more direct ways up and
down Suaineabhal, but the route
described here makes the most of the
mountain and its environs, taking in
some wild country along the way.
A walk in along the shore of Loch
Suaineabhal is followed by a cross-
country approach to the foot of the
south ridge and a long steady climb
to the cairn-marked summit with
its 360-degree vistas. The return via the
north ridge is more precipitous, but no
less enjoyable for that.

To reach the start, pass the shop and
post office at Timsgarry, continue
south along the road for 2km and then
turn left along a narrow surfaced road
at a bend (unsigned). Follow this for
1.5km alongside Loch Slacsabhat, then
turn right up a rise towards the Uig
Water Treatment Works. Park here on
the gravel area next to the road, then
head back down the road to the loch
edge and turn right along the shore of
Loch Suaineabhal, soon passing a
small jetty and boatshed.

Continue southwards along the loch
edge for 5km, following the often
vague trodden path and passing
occasional small beaches, with views of
Suaineabhal and Sneihabhal across the
loch. The going is a little rough in
places, especially where the ground
rises steeply from the loch edge, but it
presents no difficulties. At the head of
the loch there is a substantial sand and
gravel beach, and several ruins. Carry

Lewis

Loch
Riobabhat

Loch
Slacsabhat

Loch
Camasord

Euscleit
Mòr

waterworks

Loch
a' Bheannain

Loch
Suaineabhal

Suaineabhal

Sròn ri
Gaoith

Oirchleit

Sneihabhal

Loch
Gruineabhat

Lochanan
Sgeireach

0   1km

on along the beach, cross the small burn feeding into the Abhainn Chromadh an t-Sèile where it flows into the loch and head upstream along the larger burn until you can cross it easily.

Climb steadily northeastwards over rough ground to reach the Lochanan Sgeireach sitting in a shallow depression. Skirt around the southern side of the lochans and continue northeastwards to the shore of Loch Gruineabhat. Continue north along the shore, soon passing beneath the eastern flank of Sneihabhal. At the foot of the loch, climb a short way up the eroded peaty slope, bear right around the flank of Oirchleit, then ascend steadily eastwards to the bealach at the foot of Suaineabhal's southern ridge. There follows a steady 300m climb northwestwards over reasonably rough, heathery, peaty and rocky ground to the westernmost and higher (428m) of Suaineabhal's twin summits, which is marked with a stone cairn.

The isolated position makes for tremendous views in all directions, though the vista across Ardroil and Uig Sands takes some beating. On a clear day you may be lucky enough to see both the Flannan Isles to the west and St Kilda far to the southwest.

From the summit, bear northeast for a short way, then descend northwards into the obvious broad gully and follow this all the way down to a lochan sitting in the bealach below – the descent is steep and rough in places, requiring care. From the lochan, bear left (southwest) and follow the narrow path marked with wooden posts that soon descends a rough slope, heading initially towards the shore of Loch Slacasbhat before turning south past the east flank of Euscleit Mòr. Follow the posts as they steer westwards above the north shore of Loch Suaineabhal, then cross the metal bridge across the sluice dam to return to the parking area.

Crossing the bealach between
Cracabhal and Laibheal a Tuath

Uig Hills from Brèinis

Distance 12.5km **Total ascent** 940m
Time 6 hours **Terrain** rough, rocky
mountain and moorland terrain,
boggy in places; strong navigation
skills required **Map** OS Explorer 458
Access bus (W4) to Brèinis
from Stornoway

**The austerely beautiful Uig Hills
dominate the far southwest corner
of Lewis, their twin rocky ridges
arrayed either side of Gleann
Raonasgail in the north and
Gleann Tamnasdail to the south.
Beginning in the scattered coastal
township of Brèinis, this rugged
route heads south through the
rocky hills forming the seaward,
western ridge of the Uig Hills,
taking in several rocky summits,
including Mealaisbhal – the
highest summit in Lewis – before
descending the long western
ridge of Laibheal a Tuath to return
to Brèinis.**

The route is suitable for experienced
walkers with good navigation skills as
it traverses rough, pathless country

with rocky, complex terrain, which is
all part of the enjoyment of walking
in these fine hills. Needless to say, the
Uig Hills are also blessed with the
superlative views and meteorological
capriciousness that maritime
mountains often enjoy; so pack a
camera and waterproofs just in case.

Leaving the road by the old military
blockhouse at the north end of Brèinis,
follow the peat track east for 750m to
the point where it runs out amid peat
hags. Bear ENE, keeping above the
boggy terrain with Loch Sanndabhat
on your left, and then climb northeast
along the flank of Mealaisbhal before
bearing east to gain the saddle
between the rocky eminence of Mula
Mac Sgiathain and Mealaisbhal.

The direct route southwestwards to
the summit from here involves
scrambling over boulders, but this can
largely be avoided by following a
vague cairn-marked grassy path
winding its way through rocky terrain
to just below and east of the summit.
Clamber over boulders, then pick up a
path leading along the ridge's south

Islibhig

Loch Greabhat

Brèinis

Abhainn Bhreanais

Taireabhal

side to the summit, which is marked by a large cairn. On a clear day, the views from the top of Mealaisbhal are marvellous, taking in the Harris Hills to the southeast, the Flannan Isles and St Kilda to the west and southwest and Uig Sands to the north.

Leave the summit and descend the southeast ridge, picking your route carefully through rocky terrain. Make for the horseshoe-shaped Loch Dubh Gualainn an Fhirich sitting on the col at 293m (NB030260). From here, you can either climb grassy gullies up through the steeper rock on the northern slopes of Cracabhal, which looks more difficult than it actually is, or continue southwestwards from the col, keeping left of the loch as follows: pass to the left of another lochan, descend a broad gully, then skirt beneath crags towards Loch Clibh Cracabhal (NB022253). Pass to the left of the loch, then climb initially south to gain Cracabhal's west ridge. Climb northeastwards to reach the summit, marked with a pile of stones (514m).

Descend southwestwards through rocky terrain with a number of small lochans to reach a larger lochan in the col (400m) between Cracabhal and Laibheal a Tuath (NB026247). Keep to its eastern shore and climb up directly to the summit of Laibheal a Tuath (505m). Having enjoyed the expansive views, descend the long rock-scattered western ridge and at its foot bear

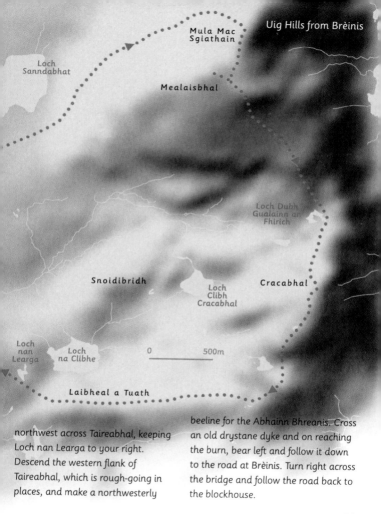

Uig Hills from Brèinis

Mula Mac Sgiathain

Loch Sanndabhat

Mealaisbhal

Loch Dubh Gualainn an Fhirich

Snoidibridh

Loch Clibh Cracabhal

Cracabhal

Loch nan Learga

Loch na Clibhe

0   500m

Laibheal a Tuath

northwest across Taireabhal, keeping Loch nan Learga to your right. Descend the western flank of Taireabhal, which is rough-going in places, and make a northwesterly beeline for the Abhainn Bhreanis. Cross an old drystane dyke and on reaching the burn, bear left and follow it down to the road at Brèinis. Turn right across the bridge and follow the road back to the blockhouse.

Uig Hills from Brèinis

Descending from Mealaisbhal with Cracabhal ahead and Tamnasbhal and Teinneasabhal across Gleann Raonasgail

Climbing Tathabhal with
Gleann Raonasgail below

16

Uig Hills from Carnish

Distance 18km **Total ascent** 950m
Time 7 hours **Terrain** rough, rocky
mountain and moorland terrain, boggy
in places **Map** OS Explorer 458
Access bus (W4) towards Brèinis from
Stornoway – ask to be let down at the
start of the Gleann Raonasgail hill track
just past Carnish

**The Uig Hills to the east of Gleann
Raonasgail are less visited than
those to the west, probably
because Mealaisbhal, the highest
hill in Lewis, is an obvious draw
for walkers and benefits from a
shorter walk in. However, this route
over Tamnasbhal, Teinneasabhal,
Tathabhal and Tarain makes for a
robust and stimulating day's walk
with grand views. While there is
less chance of encountering other
people, there is a greater chance of
seeing both golden eagles and red
deer on this side of the glen.**

The route leads into the mountains
from close-by the beautiful Uig Sands,
following a broad metalled hill track up
through Gleann Raonasgail to its high

point at the head of Gleann Tamnasdail
before climbing Tamnasbhal and the
other summits on the eastern side of
the glen, then descending back to the
glen and rejoining the track.

Park near the cattle grid just past the
Abhainn Dearg Distillery, south of
Carnish (NB033313). Pass the entrance
to a gravel pit on the left, then turn left
onto the next track. Follow it uphill,
then down to the bridge crossing the
Abhainn Stocaill and pass around a
locked gate. The track bends and
climbs as the view opens up along
Gleann Raonasgail. The track can be
seen winding up to the pass between
the ridges of rocky hills framing either
side of the glen. Pass Loch Brinneabhal
to your right and continue without
gaining much height, passing Loch Mòr
na Clibhe at the foot of Mula Mac
Sgiathain before coming alongside
Loch Reonasgail as the valley floor
narrows and the rocky mountain flanks
rise steeply on either side.

Beyond the head of the loch, the
track begins to climb with greater
purpose; continue up to the high point

Lewis

Carnish

distillery

Abhainn ... -----

Abhainn Caslabhat

Loch
Brinneabhal

Flodrasgairbhe
Mòr

Brinneabhal

Loch
Mòr na
Clibhe

Cleite
Adhamh

Loch
Reonasgail

**Mula
Sgiathan**

Tarain

Loch Mòr
Bràigh an
Tarain

Mealaisbhal

Tathabhal

Loch Suaineabhal

Gleann Tamnasdail

Cracabhal

Teinneasabhal

0   1km

**Bràigh
Buidhe**

Lochan
Dhiobadail

104

Tamnasbhal

at 263m, then leave the track. Climb steeply eastwards to the hummocky bealach at Braigh Buidhe (NB039247), with Coire Dhìobadail below to the east. From the bealach ascend the northwest ridge of Tamnasbhal to gain the summit at 467m with dramatic views down to Loch Dhìobadail. Retrace your steps to Braigh Buidhe, then continue NNE past several small lochans, climbing steadily to the summit of Teinneasbhal (497m), marked with a cairn of pink and grey granite rocks. Descend northeastwards across easier terrain, then gradually swing north towards some lochans atop the bealach (366m). Climb steeply northwards – following a grassy gully makes the going easier – to the cairn-marked summit of Tathabhal (515m), the highest hill on this side of the glen. Mealaisbhal looms directly across the glen and the views

south to the Harris Hills and the west coast are magnificent. Leave the summit bearing ENE, descending easier ground before gradually swinging north to Loch Mòr Braigh an Tarain (NB050269). Cross the outflow of the loch where it runs into a smaller lochan immediately to the east.

Continue north, climbing a gully along the right-hand side of a small burn before bearing right and continuing up through slabby rocks to the summit of Tarain Mòr (NB051277). There are excellent views north to Uig Sands. From the summit, head northeast towards Creag Stiogh an Fhais before dropping down to the lochans immediately south of Cleite Adhamh (NB050281). Descend west alongside Allt Uamha Mhircil, then cross the Abhainn Caslabhat with care to regain the Gleann Raonasgail track and return to the start.

Lewis

17

Brèinis to Tamna Siar

Distance 10km **Total ascent** 470m
Time 4 hours 30 (round trip)
Terrain exposed clifftops, rough
moorland, dense heather cover and
some boggy ground
Map OS Explorer 458 **Access** bus
(W4) to Brèinis from Stornoway,
though the nearest bus stop is in the
township itself, 3km from the start

**The coastline beyond the road
end at Brèinis in the southwest
corner of the Uig peninsula is
rugged with an austere beauty.**

The terrain is often rough and rocky
with dense heather cover; it's also
boggy in places and there are a number
of burns to cross. The vague trodden
paths are intermittent and often hard to
follow. If this all sounds a bit too much
like hard work then the upside is the
stunning coastal scenery, the views of
the Uig Hills, the Harris Hills and Eilean
Mhealasta together with the sense of
remoteness that comes just a short
distance beyond the road end. This is

Tamna Siar with the
Harris Hills beyond

107

also a good area for spotting wildlife, especially red deer and both golden and white-tailed eagles.

Although the distance isn't especially great, the going is tough in places. As this is an out-and-back linear walk there is the advantage of judging whether you walk the whole way to Tamna Siar or stop short as time, energy and enthusiasm allow. The head of the sea loch at Tamna Siar also makes for a superb camping spot and a base for exploring the headlands and hills roundabout.

At times the route passes close to sheer cliff edges and steep-sided inlets, so exercise caution.

Park carefully at the road end by the small bay at Camas Mol Linnis so as not to obstruct turning or use of the adjacent concrete slipway. There is also space for a couple of vehicles in a small lay-by 100m before the road end.

From the road end follow the intermittent trodden path southeastwards across rough, peaty ground, skirting around the stony shore at Camas Chala Moil. Follow the vague path up towards the obvious old stock fence and cross where easiest. Carry on along the fenceline and step up to the rocky clifftop with care above a vertical drop at the head of a narrow inlet. Continue on the trodden path along the clifftop, soon crossing a small burn flowing down to the inlet at Foirsgeo Geodha. Stay with the path, passing by the tunnels of an otter holt among some heathery hummocks.

The path soon arrives at the cliff edge of the sheer-sided inlet at Staca-Geodha, which shelters the pair of rock stacks that give it its name. The path follows the exposed rock of the clifftop in towards the head of the inlet. Proceed with care, stepping up along the band of exposed rock and continuing to the very top of the inlet before stepping down safely to follow the path south along the coast again. Cross the Abhainn Staca-Geodha and stay with the path as best you can. A circular drystane-walled enclosure perches on the clifftop below, while 1km across the Caolas an Eilein lies the northern end of Eilean Mhealasta with

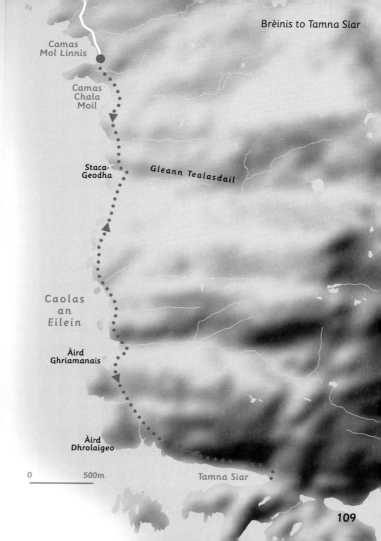

Brèinis to Tamna Siar

Camas Mol Linnis

Camas Chala Moil

Staca-Geodha

Gleann Tealasdail

Caolas an Eilein

Àird Ghriamanais

Àird Dhrolaigeo

Tamna Siar

0   500m

its enticing, steeply pitched beach.

Continue on your way, following the trodden paths where you can – the terrain is rocky and heathery and can be tough going where pathless. Stay below the craggy outcrops to landward and be careful near the clifftops. Around 1km beyond the Abhainn Staca-Geodha, you will pass Sgeir Ghlas Leac an Aiseig and another rocky outcrop connected to the shore by a narrow sandy isthmus. Cross another couple of burns, including the narrow gorge of the Linne Dhorch. The way ahead is soon funnelled down between a craggy outcrop and the rocky shore. Descend along a distinct path and step through a drystane dyke at the bottom to arrive at an area of grassy turf. Carry on along the greensward on the landward side of Àird Ghriamanais; you may need to hop over wet channels between the corrugations of old lazy beds. Cross an old drystane dyke, step over a small burn at the head of a narrow inlet and continue to landward of Àird Dhrolaigeo. Where the terrain channels down towards the narrow inlet of Geodha nan Gobhar, bear left and head up a gully, following a vague path on the right-hand side – the middle is often wet.

At the top of the gully bear southeast across the rocky, heathery terrain, following a trodden path if you can. Keep your height – above the 50m contour – as the ground drops steeply towards the sea loch below. The going is rough, but compensation comes in the views along Tamna Siar, with its jade green waters, and the Harris Hills beyond. Eventually a clearer path leads down a grassy slope to the beach and greensward at the head of Tamna Siar.

The beach is usually full of all manner of flotsam and jetsam – sadly much of it plastic, but there's usually a few interesting items to contemplate. The grassy area by the wall is ideal for pitching a tent and a burn burbles down to the shore close-by. The headlands to the south of Tamna Siar are well worth a visit if you have the time, weather and energy – otherwise it's an area that can best be explored when camping here.

Looking south to Aird Ghrìamanais

Lewis

Looking across the
sound to Eilean Mhealasta

Winter Wall at Tòb a' Ghearraidh

Àird Bheag backpack

Distance 27.5km **Total ascent** 1405m
Time 2–3 days **Terrain** rough moor
and hillcountry, mostly pathless, dense
heather cover in places and some very
boggy ground **Maps** OS Explorer 458
and 456 **Access** bus (W4) to Brèinis
from Stornoway

**At the southwesternmost corner of
Lewis, the rugged twin headlands
of Àird Bheag and Àird Mhòr lie
directly across the mouth of Loch
Rèasort from northwest Harris.
This is a beautiful place, but it is
also rough, wild country and is
a long way from the nearest road.**

Today the area south of Loch
Tamnabhaigh may seem 'empty' of
human presence, but there was a small
crofting community at Àird Bheag until
the 1960s, which is brought vividly to
life in *An Trusadh*, John MacDonald's
memoir of life here in the first half of
the 20th century. Unless you include
the hunting lodge at the head of Loch
Tamnabhaigh, the only remaining
habitation is the small crofthouse
perched above its south shore.

The route involves a walk in over the
western ridge of the Uig Hills from
Brèinis on the coast, an overnight
camp at the head of Loch Tealasbhaigh
– the sea loch between Àird Bheag and
Àird Mhòr – and a loop around the
latter headland before returning to
Brèinis. There are various ways of
approaching the Àird Bheag peninsula.
Aside from arriving by boat there are
several options for walking in and out.
The hill track between Carnish and
Tamnabhaigh is 13km each way and
the gravel surface makes for hard-going
underfoot. Despite the fine hillcountry
it passes through, it is hard to
recommend. It is also possible to walk
in around the coast from Brèinis, but
the most direct route is to cross over
from the coast near Brèinis to Ceann
Chuisil in the lee of Griomabhal –
southernmost of the Uig Hills. This last
option is the route described here.

From the road end by the slipway at
Camas Mol Linnis, south of Mèalasta,
follow the intermittent trodden path
southeastwards across rough, peaty
ground, skirting around the stony

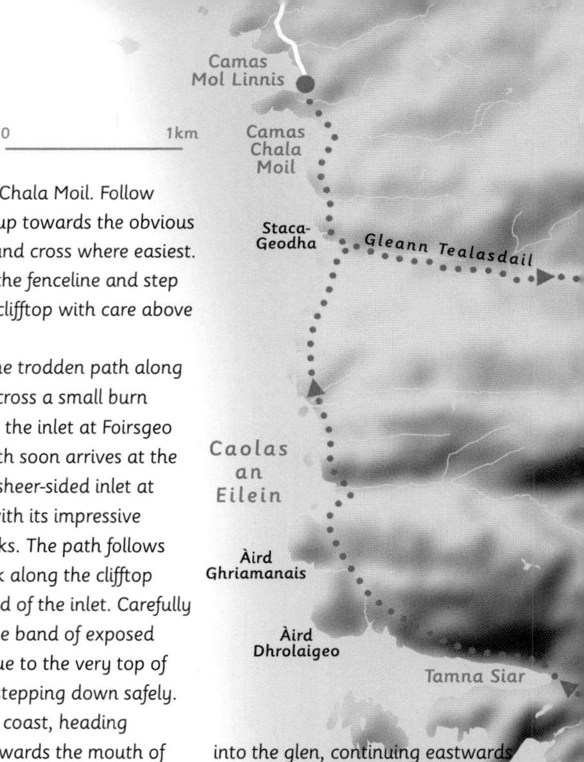

Camas
Mol Linnis

0   1km

Camas
Chala
Moil

Staca-
Geodha

Gleann Tealasdail

Caolas
an
Eilein

Àird
Ghriamanais

Àird
Dhrolaigeo

Tamna Siar

shore at Camas Chala Moil. Follow
the vague path up towards the obvious
old stock fence and cross where easiest.
Carry on along the fenceline and step
up to the rocky clifftop with care above
a vertical drop.

Continue on the trodden path along
the clifftop and cross a small burn
flowing down to the inlet at Foirsgeo
Geodha. The path soon arrives at the
cliff edge of the sheer-sided inlet at
Staca-Geodha with its impressive
pair of rock stacks. The path follows
the exposed rock along the clifftop
towards the head of the inlet. Carefully
step up along the band of exposed
rock and continue to the very top of
the inlet before stepping down safely.

Now leave the coast, heading
eastwards up towards the mouth of
Gleann Tealasdail in the lee of
Griomabhal's steep northern flank.
After 150m, cross over the Abhainn
Staca-Geodha where it flows from a
steep-sided gully. Continue up the glen
for 300m and recross the burn above
where it flows down into the gully.
Follow the Allt Gleann Tealasdail up

into the glen, continuing eastwards
towards the steep slope ahead beneath
Griomabhal's steep escarpment. At the
top of the rough, heathery slope Dubh
Loch soon comes into view, nestled in
a shallow basin to the left. Continue
straight up the narrowing glen,
following an intermittent path –
occasional marker stones or small

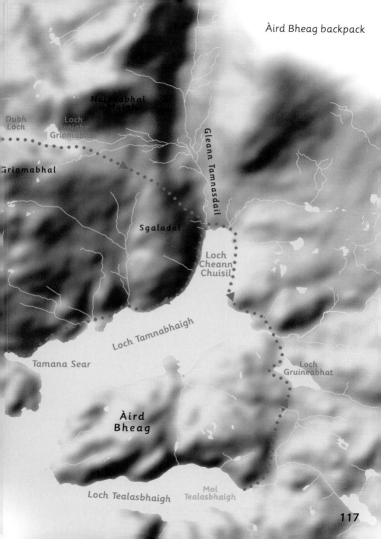

Dubh
Loch

Loch
Fhìobha
Griomabhal

Nan Eabhal
a' Chuisil

Gleann Tamnasdail

Griomabhal

Sgaladal

Loch
Cheann
Chuisil

Loch Tamnabhaigh

Tamana Sear

Loch
Gruineabhat

Àird
Bheag

Loch Tealasbhaigh

Mol
Tealasbhaigh

cairns show the way. At the head of the glen, the beautiful Loch Bràighe Griomabhal comes into view, lying between the flank of Griomabhal and the rocky summit of Naideabhal a-Muigh to the northeast.

Carry on along the southern shore of the loch, following a distinct path with more frequent marker stones. Bear right above the eastern end of the loch, keeping to the cairns and marker stones. These waymarkers are part of the route that crofter Manus Maclennan plotted from Àird Bheag to Mèalasta in the 1920s. Keep with the marker stones as they descend, gradually at first, then more steadily, following the lie of the land southeastwards down towards Ceann Chuisil. As you descend, there are fine views northeastwards across the glen to Tamnasbhal and north to Cracabhal above the head of Gleann Tamnasdail. The marker stones are easily lost as you approach the floor of Gleann Tamnasdail, but continue down the grassy slopes to the head of the loch at Ceann Chuisil, avoiding rocky outcrops.

Cross the burn and join the track leading around Loch Cheann Chuisil. Follow the track road around to Camas na Cròtha at the head of Loch Tamnabhaigh, go through the gate and pass the estate workers' bothy on the right before taking the often boggy path in front of Hamnavay Lodge down towards the Abhainn Tamnabhaig. Cross the footbridge and follow the rough trodden path up the slope, meeting the outflow of Loch Gruineabhat on the way up. The unusual drystane structure in the middle of the burn is the ruin of an old mill.

Continue up to the loch and bear right to walk anticlockwise around the shore. After 500m, at a bulge in the south shore of the loch, head south up a short slope away from the water. Walk gently downhill through a shallow glen, keeping to the right-hand side of the open ground draining into the Allt Glen Tealasavay. Keep to the right of the burn – you may have to cross peat hags further down the glen – and look out for a vague path leading to Mol Tealasbhaigh at the head of Loch Tealasbhaigh – a wild and rugged sea loch. Keep to the right-hand side of the outflow of the burn and head up through the ruins and grassy ground of an abandoned township consisting of a couple of blackhouses and a number of byres. There are good sheltered spots here for pitching a tent.

There may or may not be a stone structure or the remains thereof at the head of the loch just beyond the outflow of the burn. If there is then it's an incarnation of the 'firestacks' built, demolished by the sea, then rebuilt here by the artist, Julie Brook, in an ongoing cycle. The shoulder-high circular stacks are built from stones gathered nearby between tides; driftwood fires set on top of the stacks appear to become floating islands of fire as the tide comes in. The artist first built firestacks while living in a natural rock arch on the uninhabited northwest coast of the Isle of Jura during the early 1990s.

There are plenty of options for exploring the area from a base at Loch Tealasbhaigh. Immediately to the southwest lies Àird Mhòr and the headland can be walked in a couple of hours or so (see page 123).

To return to Brèinis either retrace your outward route or alternatively return to Ceann Chuisil and then head around the coast as follows.

At the head of the loch, by some ruined shielings, cross the outflow of the Abhainn Cheann Chuisil by hopping across rocks to continue around the coast. However, the river can be difficult to cross in spate, so it may be wise to cross higher up after heavy rain. Once you're across, walk around the edge of the loch just above the shore on the rough, heathery slopes beneath Sgaladal. Initially, there are vague traces of path to follow and these become more defined as you progress. There is an exposed section of path by the small stony beach at the mouth of Gleann Sgaladail and a burn must also be crossed here.

Beyond the next small bay, avoid the precipitously steep section of coastline by crossing up and over the neck of Meall Arsbaig. Continue above the shore to the inlet of Tamana Sear, then cut across the neck of the headland, following the course of an old drystane dyke to the west-facing inlet of Tamna Siar. A patch of grassy ground sitting above the head of the inlet makes for an excellent place to pitch a tent and it also benefits from a freshwater spring and plenty of driftwood. However, being west-facing, it's not ideal for camping if there's a gale blowing in off the Atlantic.

From Tamna Siar, the way along the north side of the inlet is difficult and hazardous close to the shore, so climb to around 50m, keeping a lookout for a vague path, which can be followed much of the way to the road head south of Mèalasta. Pick your route carefully as there are some rocky sections to negotiate and the ground is rough, boggy and heathery; by way of compensation the dramatic coastal landscape is quite spectacular. Continue around the coast to the inlet on the south side of the rocky headlands of Àird Dhrolaigeo and Àird Ghriaminais, then follow the path cutting across the low-lying neck of the headlands.

Emerging on the west coast of the Uig peninsula, there are splendid views across the narrow Caolas an Eilein onto Eilean Mhealasta with an appealing sandy beach at its northeastern end. Carefully follow the path along and above the shore, traversing a few rocky sections and crossing several burns – the coastal scenery here is magnificent. Eventually you will arrive at the road head near Mèalasta.

Heading up the glen from Tòb a' Ghèarraidh

Àird Bheag backpack

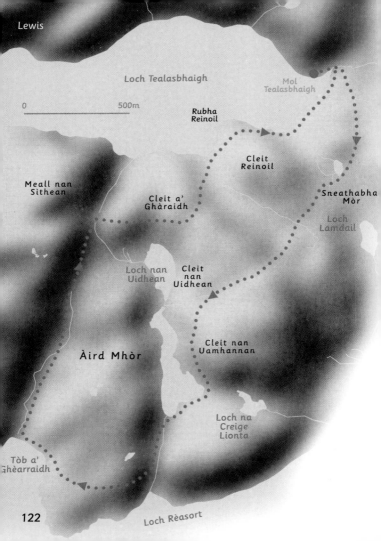

Lewis

Loch Tealasbhaigh

Mol
Tealasbhaigh

0   500m

Rubha
Reinoil

Cleit
Reinoil

Meall nan
Sithean

Cleit a'
Ghàraidh

Sneathabha
Mòr

Loch
Lamdail

Loch nan
Uidhean

Cleit
nan
Uidhean

Àird Mhòr

Cleit nan
Uamhannan

Loch na
Creige
Lionta

Tòb a'
Ghèarraidh

Loch Rèasort

Around Àird Mhòr

Distance 6.5km **Total ascent** 305m
Time 2 hours 30

From the head of Loch Tealasbhaigh, either cross the outflow of the burn or walk upstream and cross where safe to do so. Climb south up the rough peaty slope with the bulk of Sneathabhal Mòr to the left and the rocky outcrop of Cleit Reinoil to the right. Pass a lochan and then bear right to continue across peaty open ground. Make for the obvious gap atop a slope between the rocky flanks of Cleit nan Uidhean and Cleit nan Uamhannan. Head down the gully on the other side, keeping right to avoid the worst of the wet ground.

Nestled in the glen below Loch nan Uidhean comes into view, separated by a narrow isthmus. As the gully opens out bear south and continue along the hillside above the loch without losing too much height. There are good views ahead across Loch Rèasort with the rocky eminence of Taran Mòr rising steeply from the loch edge.

Drop to the end of the loch, cross the outflow and follow the burn before trending southwest, then west to cut across the promontory of Rubha nan Uan into the bay at Tòb a' Gèarraidh. A circular stone-walled structure comes into view above the shore on the east side of the glen. The pale newness of the stone, the symmetry of the stonework and the narrow cleft on the loch-facing aspect point to this being the work of Julie Brook. By contrast the ruinous lichen-clad remains of several beehive cells are found nearby.

Head north up the glen, sticking to the right-hand side of the burn as you climb. Keep to the left-hand side of the glen higher up and when the gradient eases contour along the flank of Meall nan Sìthean to arrive at a boggy bealach with views north across Loch Tealasbhaigh. Head east along the south side of Cleit a' Ghàraidh for 500m, then at an obvious gap to the northwest of Cleit nan Uidhean descend rough sloping ground towards the coast at Rubha Reinoil. Cross a burn, continue around the flank of Cleit Reinoil, then follow the rough loch edge back to the head of Loch Tealasbhaigh.

Following the Abhainn a' Lòin through the strath

19

Morsgail Forest

Distance 18.5km **Total ascent** 300m
Time 6 hours **Terrain** rough, tussocky
moorland terrain, very boggy in places;
potentially tricky river crossing
Maps OS Explorer 458 and 456
Access bus (W4) to Giosla (Gisla) from
Stornoway. The Westside Circular
Clockwise morning service (W2) from
Stornoway connects with the W4 at
Garynahine (Gearraidh na h-Aibhne)

**The Morsgail Forest lies in the
strath – a broad, shallow river
valley – between the heads of tidal
Loch Ròg Beag and 9km-long Loch
Rèasort, which forms the western
boundary between Lewis and
Harris. It is a 'deer forest', used for
stalking by the Morsgail Estate
rather than a wooded area.**

The Loidse Mhorsgail hunting lodge
sits next to Loch Morsgail near the
northern end of the valley while at
Ceann Loch Reasort to the south a
boarded-up house and an estate bothy
sit either side of the head of the loch
with the Harris Hills providing a
magnificent backdrop. In between, the
Abhainn a' Lòin meanders northwards
from the watershed while a series of
lochs lie in Srath Bàn to the south.
The whole of the strath can be quite
boggy, the southern stretch especially
so – gaiters or wellington boots are
recommended. Negotiating the often
soggy terrain is well worth the effort
for the exceptional beehive dwellings at
Gearraidh Bheinn na Gile alone and the
remarkable landscape at the head of
Loch Rèasort certainly justifies the bog-
trotting en route.

Although this is a low-level route
it does have its challenges, namely
boggy ground, potentially tricky river
crossings and intermittent paths –
especially further south. Ideally, this
route is best walked during a period
of dry weather. Navigation can also
be tricky, hence this is not a walk to
undertake in poor visibility.

Park by the side of the road near the
gate across the road to Morsgail
Lodge, being careful not to cause any
obstruction. Follow the track road for
1.5km as it winds its way alongside the
river with its series of weirs – if the river

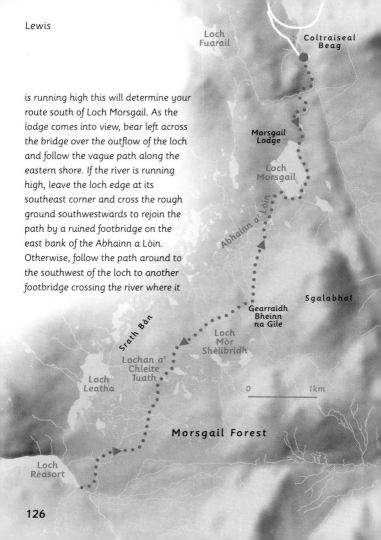

Lewis

is running high this will determine your route south of Loch Morsgail. As the lodge comes into view, bear left across the bridge over the outflow of the loch and follow the vague path along the eastern shore. If the river is running high, leave the loch edge at its southeast corner and cross the rough ground southwestwards to rejoin the path by a ruined footbridge on the east bank of the Abhainn a Lòin. Otherwise, follow the path around to the southwest of the loch to another footbridge crossing the river where it

Loch Fuarail

Coltraiseal Beag

Morsgail Lodge

Loch Morsgail

Abhainn a' Lòin

Sgalabhal

Gearraidh Bheinn na Gile

Loch Mòr Shèlibridh

Srath Bàn

Lochan a' Chleite Tuath

Loch Leatha

0   1km

Morsgail Forest

Loch Rèasort

flows into the loch. Turn left alongside the river, climbing a little over a rocky outcrop, soon joining the path that runs along the western side of Loch Morsgail to the north. Turn south (left) along the path and continue along the riverbank. Pass another weir and continue to the stone-built abutments where a footbridge once stood. Cross here to the eastern bank of the Abhainn a Lòin if safe to do so. Otherwise continue upstream to a weir made from gabions — wire cages full of boulders — and cross here if safe to do so. Follow the intermittently boggy ATV track south across the moorland below the western slopes of Sgalabhal for 1.25km, ignoring two right-hand branches before reaching Gearraidh Bheinn na Gile.

Here, by the Abhainn Bheinn na Gile, is a cluster of beehive shielings, comprising three adjoining cells, the outer two now roofless, the inner cell with roof intact. It has two low, lintelled entrances, one west-facing, the other opening into the inter-communicating cell. The building date is not known, but it likely pre-dates the 19th-century Clearances and would have been used seasonally, when livestock were moved to upland grazing. Similar dwellings are found throughout the Hebrides, Ireland and beyond; built with the materials to hand, using ancient techniques dating back to Neolithic times to construct effective weatherproof shelters. The lower courses of stone were laid horizontally while the upper courses were corbelled, overlapping in decreasing circles and capped with a coping stone. The exterior would be clad with turfs to windproof and waterproof the shelter. It is well worth crawling inside the roofed cell for a look around.

Cross the burn on the makeshift footbridge a little downstream, then bear left along the ATV track, heading southwest. Ignore the pale marker posts — at least on the outward leg. The terrain can be very boggy here — old tyres have been laid to give ATVs purchase in the soft ground. Cross another ford through the burn flowing down from Loch Mòr Shèlibridh. Continue southwestwards on the intermittent path, negotiating fords across the outflow of Lochan a' Chleite Tuath and the Allt a' Chleite Tuath. The track is broad, but remains difficult to follow at times where it fades into the terrain. Carry on down towards Ceann Loch Reasort as the view opens out across the Harris Hills with the distinctive overhanging buttress of Sròn Uladail prominent to the southwest. It's easy to lose the track amid the peat hags above the head of the loch, but continue on your southwesterly course and you will soon arrive at Ceann Loch Reasort.

There is no longer a bridge across the Abhainn Mhòr Ceann Reasoirt where it flows into the loch, but it is possible to cross dry-shod by the shingle banks at the head of the loch if the river is not in spate. An abandoned metal-roofed house stands above the north shore while across the river a small white-painted house is used as a bothy by the Rèasort estates.

Either return by your outward route or look out for the marker stones and occasional pale marker posts indicating a pathless route across the moorland that was created by the former postman, Callum Macaskill. After 47 years of walking the route from Morsgail three times a week to collect and deliver the mail around the head of Loch Rèasort, Callum was awarded a British Empire Medal on his retirement. The frequent marker stones plot a fairly straight course, but they cross some rough, boggy ground with plenty of peat hags. This route does make for a change from the ATV track, however.

Beehive dwelling at Gearraidh Bheinn na Gile

Cairn on Mula Chlainn Neil, Liuthaid

20

Liuthaid and Mullach a' Ruisg

Distance 11km **Total ascent** 570m
Time 4 hours **Terrain** good paths for
the walk in and out; pathless, grassy
hill terrain with heather cover and
wet ground on the hillsides
Map OS Explorer 456 **Access** bus
(W10) between Tarbert and Stornoway
– ask to be let down at the Bowglass
parking area at the mouth of
Glen Bhìogadail

**The 'border' between Harris and
Lewis traverses the ridgeline of
Liuthaid and Mullach a' Ruisg on
its way over to Gleann Langadail
where it recruits the immense
freshwater Loch Langabhat (the
Long Loch) to do some of its
boundary work for it.**

The route described here crosses
between Lewis and Harris as it takes
in Liuthaid's twin summits – Mula
Chlainn Neil and Mullach Bhìogadail
respectively – and the summit of
Mullach a' Ruisg. The border is left
behind before it dives down into Glen
Langadail in favour of returning to the
start through Glen Bhìogadail. As these

hills form an outlying ridge the route
has grand views in all directions, not
least those of Loch Seaforth and the
hills of the Clisham Horseshoe. There
is also a good chance of seeing some
wildlife, including mountain hares,
red deer and golden eagles.

From the parking area at the mouth
of Glen Bhìogadail, follow the path
along the right-hand side of the A859
for 1.3km to Loidse Ath Linne. Cross
the road with care to go over a stile
in a fence next to a stock gate with
a sign reading 'Fáilte Air Luchd
Coiseachd – Walkers Welcome'. Head
northwestwards up the track leading
to Loch Langabhat for around 2km to
just below the bealach where there
are ruined shielings at Airigh Lag a'
Chrotha – these are only shown on
the OS Explorer map and are hardly
apparent on the ground. Find a safe
place to cross the burns feeding the
Abhainn a' Mhuil, then begin the steep
300m climb up the heathery, often
wet hillside that ultimately leads to
the cairn-marked summit of Mula
Chlainn Neil (492m), Liuthaid's

northernmost summit. The climb is
fairly unrelenting, but your reward
comes in the splendid views southeast
along Loch Seaforth, and south and
west onto the Harris Hills.

In contrast to the preceding uphill
slog, it is a gentle stroll south to gain
Mullach Bhiogadail – Liuthaid's
southern summit. From here, follow
the intermittent line of metal fenceposts
running southwest to the stone pile
cairn marking the summit of Mullach
a' Ruisg (473m).

Mula
Chlainn
Neil

Liuthaid

Mullach
Bhiogada

0   500m

Mullach
a' Ruisg

Glen Langadail

Tom
Ruisg

Loch
Ruisg

Bealach na
h-Uamha

Glen Bhiogadail

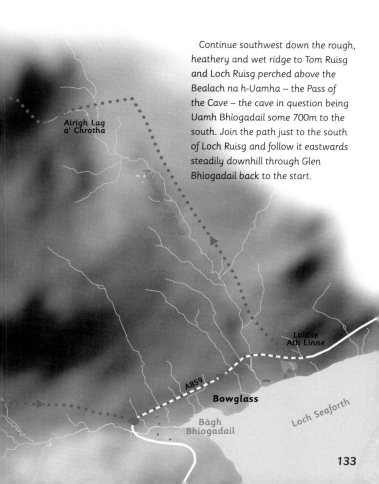

Continue southwest down the rough, heathery and wet ridge to Tom Ruisg and Loch Ruisg perched above the Bealach na h-Uamha – the Pass of the Cave – the cave in question being Uamh Bhìogadail some 700m to the south. Join the path just to the south of Loch Ruisg and follow it eastwards steadily downhill through Glen Bhìogadail back to the start.

Airigh Lag a' Chrotha

Abhainn a' Ghlinne

Loidse Ath Linne

A859

Bowglass

Bàgh Bhìogadail

Loch Seaforth

On Beinn na h Uamha with Loch Sealg beyond

21

The northern hills of Pàirc

Distance 19km **Total ascent** 1130m
Time 8 hours **Terrain** rough mountain
and moorland terrain, boggy in places
Map OS Explorer 457 **Access** no bus to
the start; the nearest stop is the South
Lochs turn on the Stornoway to Tarbert
(W2) service, 5.75km from the route

**Much of the remote hillcountry
of Pàirc is only accessible to
backpackers or those arriving and
departing by sea, while climbing
the area's highest hill, Beinn Mhòr,
requires a long walk in and out.
However, the northernmost hills
of Pàirc are accessible from the
road at Ceann Shiphoirt – the
head of Loch Seaforth.**

A walk taking in the hills forming the
flanks of the glen through which the
Abhainn Sgeireabhat flows and those
at its head makes for a substantial
outing, traversing six summits (or
seven with a small detour). The route is
almost entirely pathless, rough-going
and boggy in places, but with some
easier walking along the ridges and
fabulous views to boot.

Park in the small lay-by just before
the bridge at Ceann Shìphoirt. From
the lay-by, go over the bridge and
follow the road, crossing the Abhainn
Sgeireabhat and then continuing for
another 50m to where a small burn
flows through a culvert under the road.
Follow the burn up through the grass
and heather of Geàrraidh Sgeiravat,
gaining height along the flank of the
rugged ridge framing the eastern side
of the glen, with the rocky summit of
Feiriosbhal ahead to the south.

Carry on, climbing more steeply
alongside the course of the burn,
trending southeastwards up through
the hollow of Lagan Dubh to gain the
saddle between Creag na h-Uamha
and Feiriosbhal. Continue southwards
along the rocky ridge to the summit
of Feiriosbhal (327m), marked with
a rough stone-built trig point. There
are fine views all round, including
southeastwards to Loch Sealg beyond
Eishken. Descend southwards, pass a
couple of lochans and carry on along
the ridge, soon climbing to the summit
of Beinn Mheadhanach (288m) with

Loch Àirigh Thormoid and smaller Clàr
Loch in the glen below to the west.
Descend southwestwards towards the
southeastern extremity of Clàr Loch.
Join the old gravel stalkers' path
briefly, cross a footbridge and then
head southwest. Cross a deep, narrow
burn with care and pass by Loch Fath,
making for the rocky eminence of
Creag na h-Uamha.

Climb the rough slope to the bealach
immediately east of Creag na h-Uamha
and climb westwards, avoiding the
craggy terrain on its northern flank.
Loch Raoineabhat comes into view
below as you climb to gain the
northeast ridge of Beinn na h-Uamha.
The cairn-marked lower top is reached
at 366m and a brief down and up
brings you to the summit cairn at
389m. Muaitheabhal lies ahead, WSW
across the Briseadh Mhuaithabhal,
while to the southwest Beinn Mhòr
looms imposingly across Gleann Airigh
an Domhnuill. Descend westwards to
the bealach but keep to its north side
to avoid the worst of some impressive
peat hags. Climb west, then southwest

136

The northern hills of Pàirc

Loch Seaforth

Tòb MhicColla

Ceann Shiphoirt

Abhainn Sgeireabhat

Creag na h-Uamha

Feiriosbhal

Loch Àirigh Thormoid

Beinn Mheadhanach

Clàr Loch

Loch Fath

Pàirc

Creag na h-Uamha

Loch na Beirighe

0   1km

Loch Raoineabhat

along the northeast ridge to reach the summit of Muaitheabhal at 424m, with grand views onto the north flank of Beinn Mhòr directly to the south. Guaineamol and Mòr-Mhonadh lie to the northeast across the head of Gleann na h-Uamha and this vantage point provides a good opportunity to familiarise yourself with the onward route.

From the summit, return NNE along the ridge and continue steadily northwards down the northern flank of Muaitheabhal to the bealach below. Now do the opposite and climb steadily at length up the southern flank of Guaineamol. Bear northeastwards at the top of the climb to reach the cairn-marked summit (406m). Guaineamol and its neighbouring hills are known in some parts of Lewis and Harris as the Cailleach na Mointeach, or Old Woman of the Moors, because the profile when viewed from the west resembles a sleeping woman – an impression enhanced by the 'nose' atop the summit of Sidhean an Airgid,

lying immediately to the northwest of Guaineamol.

If you have the energy, drop to the northwest to cross a saddle and climb to the summit of Sidhean an Airgid before returning via the northern flank of Guaineamol to continue along the ridge. Otherwise continue eastwards from Guaineamol to an unnamed top at spot height 388m, then bear northeast and make for the cairn-marked summit of Mòr-Mhonadh (401m). Continue north to an unnamed cairn-marked top (380m) before descending steadily northeastwards, initially along the ridge, then trending eastwards towards a bealach at spot height 189m to the south of Cùl Chreag. Carry on descending a little north of eastwards over rough ground, aiming for an old ATV track running parallel to the Abhainn Sgeireabhat north of the outflow from Loch Àirigh Thormoid. Follow the path, which can be boggy after wet weather, through the glen back to Ceann Shìphoirt.

Cairn on the summit of
Beinn na h-Uamha
with Beinn Mhòr on the left
and The Clisham to the right

Looking down to Ceann Loch Shealg

22

Loch Sealg from Eishken

Distance 13.75km **Total ascent** 350m
Time 4 hours 30 **Terrain** rough
moorland terrain, paths for much
of the way, boggy in places
Map OS Explorer 457 **Access** no bus
to the start

**Cutting into the wild and remote
hillcountry at the heart of Pàirc,
Loch Sealg stretches for 8km from
the east coast to Ceann Loch
Shealg at the mouth of Gleann
Airigh an Domhnuill.**

The north shore is punctuated by a
series of tidal inlets and anchorages –
at the fishing village of Lemreway
towards the mouth of the loch, the
small township of Orinsay, the
abandoned village of Stiomrabhaigh
and Eishken towards the head of the
loch where the Eishken Lodge is found.
On the south side there is only empty
shoreline rising to the wild, hilly
hinterland. This is a propitious area for
wildlife spotting; as well as its large
population of red deer, Pàirc has a
significant population of breeding
golden eagles and there are also
nesting white-tailed eagles. The path
from Eishken along Loch Sealg
contours above the shore, providing
good views across the loch, so look out
for seals, otters, waders and divers.

Starting from Eishken, the route
follows track and path to Ceann Loch
Shealg, then continues into Gleann
Airigh an Domhnuill before crossing
rough, wet ground over a bealach and
returning to Eishken on a good stalkers'
path through Gleann Cheothadail.
(Walking out and back to Ceann Loch
Shealg makes a shorter, easier option.)

From the parking area, walk down
the road towards the lodge, bearing
left alongside metal railings and going
through an electric gate leading into
the grounds of Eishken Lodge. Bear
right past the nursery and hedge-
enclosed garden, then turn right past
the front of the lodge and continue
through another gate. The track
initially leads down the west side of
Tòb Eisgein, then bears west – look out
for the estate ponies that can often be
found here. The route continues above
the north shore of Loch Sealg, passing

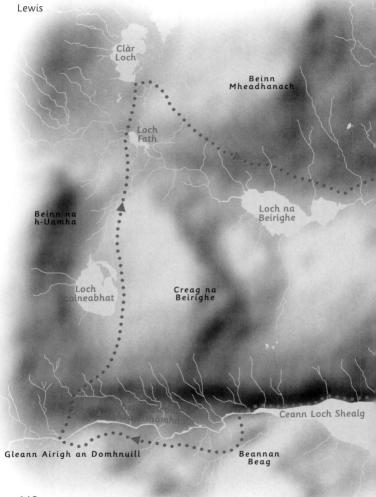

Lewis

Clàr Loch

Beinn Mheadhanach

Loch Fath

Beinn na h-Uamha

Loch na Beirighe

Loch aoineabhat

Creag na Beirighe

Ceann Loch Shealg

Gleann Airigh an Domhnuill

Beannan Beag

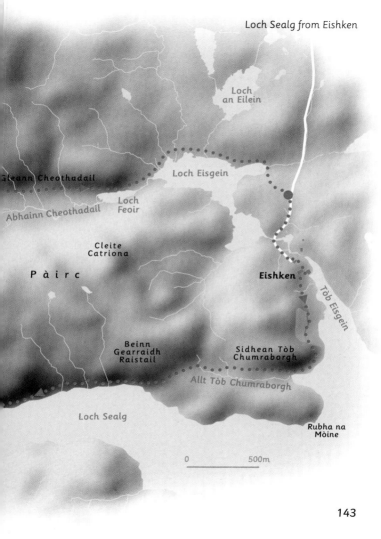

Loch Sealg from Eishken

Loch
an Eilein

Gleann Cheothadail

Loch Eisgein

Loch
Feoir

Abhainn Cheothadail

Cleite
Catriona

Pàirc

Eishken

Tòb Eisgein

Beinn
Gearraidh
Raistail

Sidhean Tòb
Chumraborgh

Allt Tòb Chumraborgh

Loch Sealg

Rubha na
Mòine

0   500m

through a gate in a deer fence. The track narrows to a path but remains distinct if muddy in places, crossing several culverted burns and a couple of footbridges on the way to Ceann Loch Shealg.

The wreck of a small vessel, the *Ensis*, lies at the head of the loch and on the south shore is the abandoned township of Ceann Loch Shealg, which was cleared in the mid-19th century. Cross the footbridge over the Abhainn Gleann Airighean Dhòmhnaill, continue for 200m to a path junction and turn right to take the gravel stalkers' path westwards below Beannan Mòr. Bear right at a junction and follow the path down to recross the Abhainn Gleann Airighean Dhòmhnaill. A footbridge is marked on the OS map here, but it is no longer there. Find a safe place to cross – which may require heading upstream, depending on how high and fast the burn is flowing.

Head northeast up the rough slope to the bealach between Beinn na h-Uamha and Creag na Beirighe. Pass to the east of Loch Raoineabhat where the going is rough and often boggy. Descend northwards from the bealach and cross the burns flowing into Loch Fath. Continue northwards towards Clàr Loch and pick up the old gravel stalkers' path. Turn right and head southeast along the moss-covered path, climbing at first and then descending steadily past Loch na Beirighe towards its eastern end. Continue alongside the Abhainn Cheothadail through the eponymous glen. Pass Loch Feoir, go through a rickety rope-tied gate and continue to the western tip of Loch Eisgein where the good path gives way to an old ATV track running along the north shore of the loch. Pick up the path through a gap in a fence, cross a couple of small fords and continue to the eastern end of the loch. Bear right here, cross the burn flowing into the loch and pick up the ATV track running back to the parking area by the road at Eishken.

Waterfall at Ceann Loch Shealg

Loch Sealg from Eishken

145

Beinn Mhòr from Bràigh an Fhorsa

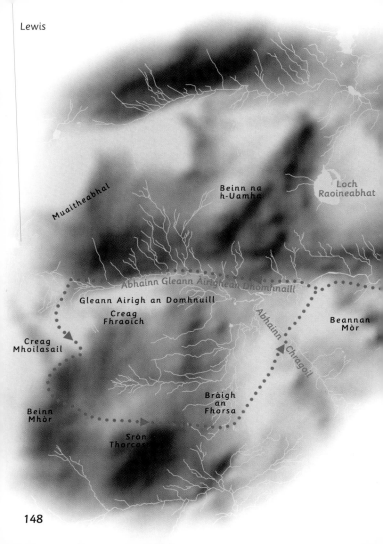

Beinn Mhòr

Distance 21km **Total ascent** 900m **Time** 8 hours 30 **Terrain** rough mountain and moorland terrain, boggy in places **Map** OS Explorer 457 **Access** no bus to the start; the nearest stop is the South Lochs turn on the Stornoway to Tarbert (W2) service, 7km from the route

The Pàirc region of southeast Lewis is a landscape of rough, rolling hillcountry, moorland and rugged coastline riven by a series of long sea lochs. It is a huge area of land all but cut off from the rest of Lewis by the ingress of Loch Seaforth to the south and Loch Erisort to the north. The summit of Beinn Mhòr makes a fine vantage point for surveying the hinterland of Pàirc and the western seaboard across The Minch.

The northern part of Pàirc is home to 11 scattered townships and a population of 400 while the area south of Loch Sealg (pronounced 'Shell') has been devoid of inhabitants since the land was cleared during the early 19th century. Such an expanse of wild land is of course good for wildlife. As well as a large population of red deer, Pàirc has one of the highest densities of breeding golden eagles in Europe and there are also nesting white-tailed eagles.

At 572m, Beinn Mhòr is Lewis' second highest hill (after Mealaisbhal, at 574m, in the Uig Hills). This is a long and rewarding walk through some fine wild landscapes; the walk in and out benefits from tracks and paths alongside Loch Sealg and through Gleann Airigh an Domhnuill, whereas the ascent and descent of Beinn Mhòr traverses rough, pathless country and navigation can be tricky if visibility is poor.

From the parking area in Eishken, walk down the road towards the lodge, bearing left alongside metal railings and going through an electric gate leading into the grounds of Eishken Lodge. Bear right past the nursery and hedge-enclosed garden, then turn right past the front of the lodge and continue through another gate.

Lewis

Muaitheabhal

Beinn na
h-Uamha

Loch
Raoineabhat

Abhainn Gleann Airighean Dhomhnaill

Gleann Airigh an Domhnuill

Creag
Fhraoich

Creag
Mhoilasail

Abhainn Chragoil

Beannan
Mòr

Beinn
Mhòr

Bràigh
an
Fhorsa

Sròn
Thorcasdail

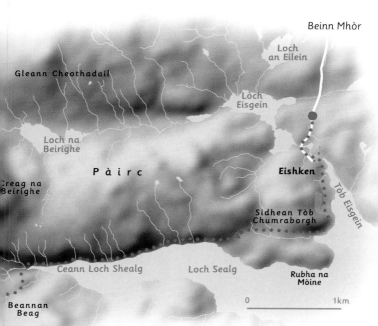

Beinn Mhòr

Loch an Eilein

Gleann Cheothadail

Loch Eisgein

Loch na Beirighe

Pàirc

Creag na Beirighe

Eishken

Tòb Eisgein

Sidhean Tòb Chumraborgh

Ceann Loch Shealg

Loch Sealg

Rubha na Mòine

Beannan Beag

0   1km

The track initially leads down the west side of Tòb Eisgein, then bears west – look out for the estate ponies that can often be found here. The route continues above the north shore of Loch Sealg, passing through a gate in a deer fence. The track narrows to a path but remains distinct, if muddy in places, crossing several culverted burns and a couple of footbridges on the way to Ceann Loch Shealg.

The wreck of a small vessel, the *Ensis*,

lies at the head of the loch and on the south shore is the abandoned township of Ceann Loch Shealg, which was cleared in the mid-19th century. Cross the footbridge over the Abhainn Gleann Airighean Dhòmhnaill, continue for 200m to a path junction and turn right to take the gravel stalkers' path westwards below Beannan Mòr. Bear right at a junction and follow the path down to recross the Abhainn Gleann Airighean Dhòmhnaill. A footbridge is

149

marked on the OS map, but it is no longer there. Find a safe place to cross – which may require heading further upstream, depending on how high and fast the burn is flowing.

Continue westwards on rough, occasionally boggy ground; look out for an intermittent path that climbs gently up through the glen, crossing several watercourses flowing into the burn as you progress. A grassier area with the ruins of old shielings is reached after around 1.5km at Airigh an Domhnuill. Continue climbing more steadily for a further 1km to reach the bealach between Muaitheabhal and Beinn Mhòr at the head of the glen.

From the bealach, head directly southwest, following a burn up a broad gully. At the head of the gully bear SSE to climb through a long corrie, crossing several slabs in its upper reaches before gaining the northeast ridge of Beinn Mhòr. Follow the ridge, which is a bit bouldery in its upper reaches, to gain

the summit marked at 572m by Carnan Sheoruis. The views across the wild empty hinterland of Pàirc and out across The Minch to the mountainous mainland are tremendous.

Head south a short way before bearing southeast to descend Beinn Mhòr's sweeping southeast ridge. Descend steadily as far as Sròn Thorcasmol, then bear east and descend more steeply into Bràigh an Fhorsa. Make for the northern end of the largest of several lochans – the ground can be boggy here – then bear northeast and gain a little height. Contour around the hillside at around 150m and you will eventually reach a gravel track with a trout-shaped weather vane at its terminus. Follow the path as it gently descends into Gleann Airigh an Domhnuill, passing the sharp turning where you crossed the Abhainn Gleann Airighean Dhòmhnaill on the outward leg. Retrace the route back to Eishken.

Beinn Mhòr from Beinn na h-Uamha

Beinn Mhòr

Ruin at Stiomrabhaigh overlooking
Lodan Stiomrabhaigh

Stiomrabhaigh

Distance 5km (round trip)
Total ascent 200m **Time** 2 hours
(round trip) **Terrain** rough, heathery
moorland terrain, boggy in places
Map OS Explorer 457 **Access** although
there is a bus service, it is not possible
to travel to and from Orinsay by bus
on the same day

**Tucked away beside a narrow inlet
off Loch Sealg in the sparsely
populated Pàirc region of southeast
Lewis, the verdant terrain and
ruinous remains of the abandoned
village of Stiomrabhaigh are both
poignant and beautiful.**

The township has been deserted since
the 1940s, but though the people have
long gone there is still much to see
here: ruined houses, dilapidated byres,
tumbledown enclosures and the
corrugations of old lazy beds – like an
empty stage set in an abandoned
theatre. In 1851, Stiomrabhaigh had
16 dwellings and a population of 81.
By this time, many settlements in Pàirc
had already been cleared to make way
for sheep, but the crofters of

Stiomrabhaigh had the security of
leasing their land directly from the
landowner. However, in 1857 when
their leases expired, the community
accepted the offer of crofts in
Lemreway a short distance to the east
and Stiomrabhaigh was abandoned.
In 1921 crofters returned to the
township, but these settlers never
gained official recognition nor any
support and, crucially, no road was
ever built to Stiomrabhaigh. Over the
next couple of decades, settlers
returned to Lemreway and by the end
of the 1940s Stiomrabhaigh was
deserted once again.

Stiomrabhaigh is the most easily
accessible of Pàirc's abandoned
townships at less than 2km from the
road at Orinsay. Although the distance
isn't great, the terrain is rough in
places and prone to bogginess, so this
short walk is not to be taken too
lightly. Walking boots with gaiters are
advisable during or after wet weather.
There is a good chance of spotting
white-tailed eagles in the area.

If driving, continue through Orinsay

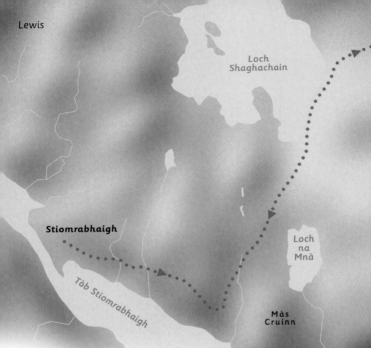

Lewis

Loch
Shaghachain

Stiomrabhaigh

Tòb Stiomrabhaigh

Loch
na
Mnà

Màs
Cruinn

and park carefully and considerately beyond the cattle grid (NB361120). The start of the route is 300m south of the cattle grid at a picnic area with an interpretation panel and map. Climb the steps here and follow the path uphill between fences to a gate. Go through and bear right to follow the marker posts contouring around the northern side of the hill along the

fenceline (there is also a less-frequented path branching left to climb over Gieàrol). Continue around to the eastern shore of Loch Shaghachain, then bear southwest to cross boggy open moorland towards Loch Sealg. The ground becomes firmer and the path more defined as you continue, trending westwards above and then descending towards Tòb Stiomrabhaigh

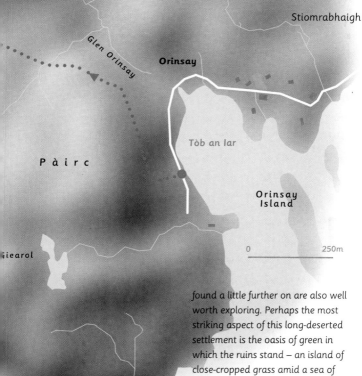

Stiomrabhaigh

Glen Orinsay

Orinsay

Tòb an Iar

Pàirc

Orinsay
Island

ìearol

0   250m

– the mouth of the inlet where the ruins
of the abandoned township lie.

The first house is the most intact
and the remains of a number of other
houses, sheep fanks and lazy beds

found a little further on are also well
worth exploring. Perhaps the most
striking aspect of this long-deserted
settlement is the oasis of green in
which the ruins stand – an island of
close-cropped grass amid a sea of
heather and moor grass; testament to
the years of crofting here, now long
past. A stand of aspens growing from a
crag below the first ruins – out of the
reach of deer and sheep – adds to the
verdant incongruity of the place. Take
the time to explore the ruins and their
environs before returning to Orinsay.

Lewis

Looking across Loch nam Bodach to Cnoc Dubh

Cuairt Cromor

Distance 4km **Total ascent** 150m
Time 2 hours **Terrain** rocky and
heathery moorland terrain, boggy in
places **Map** OS Explorer 457
Access bus (W9) to Cromor from
Stornoway, though connections and
times are of limited use

**Near the northeastern tip of the
South Lochs area of southeast
Lewis, the small coastal village
of Cromore is scattered along a
winding road through a landscape
of lochs and heather-clad hillocks.**

Immediately to the east of the
settlement lies an area of low rocky
hills, rugged coastline, and freshwater
and tidal lochs. An established walking
route around this rough terrain is
known as Cuairt Cromor – the Cromor
Circuit. This short circular walk is
waymarked by wooden posts with
yellow-painted tops. Several high
points along the way provide grand
views along the coast and – on a clear
day – across The Minch to the
mainland mountains.

Towards the end of the route the
outflow of tidal Loch nam Bodach
presents a serious obstacle, only
negotiable at low tide. The channel is
knee deep and full of slippery rocks
and broken mussel shells, so removing
footwear to get across is not an option.
Walking poles are indispensable and
wellington boots are recommended.
However, there is no need to take
any risks with this crossing as an
enjoyable detour can be made around
Loch nam Bodach.

Parking is limited, but there is
space on the verge opposite the red
phonebox; take care not to block
access or passing places. Continue to
the end of the road, passing an
information panel for the walk on the
left. Turn right between a garage and a
barn to follow a grassy path up to a
gate. Go through the gate into the field
with a large ruined house and turn
right to follow the fence to a gate in the
corner. Go through this and turn left
uphill between fences to reach a
wooden marker post.

Follow a faint trodden path through
the heather with the fence on your left.

Bear left of some rocky outcrops to reach a marker post on the summit of Meall an Nònach (53m), with good views northeast to the Eye Peninsula, east of Stornoway. Descend quite steeply to cross the wet ground above the shore at Camas Aspaic and head steeply uphill, following marker posts. On gaining the ridge, bear right (south) and carry on towards the next – unnamed – high point (73m) with Loch Dubh below to the right. There are good views across the small islands immediately to the east and, on a clear day, the mountains on the mainland. Continue down along the rough, rocky ridge, following the intermittent grassy path through the heather with tidal Loch nam Bodach ahead.

From the top of the next rocky outcrop (marked as The Ròdh on the OS Explorer map), follow the vague path southeastwards down towards the causeway linking Cuairt Cromor with the tidal island of Eilean Orasaidh. It is possible to cross to the island at low tide, otherwise continue southwards, following the marker posts climbing to the top of the next rocky hillock, Cnoc Dubh (56m). From the summit, it appears that the spit of land projecting eastwards from the far side of Loch nam Bodach provides a way across, which it does not. Instead, continue southwest, making for the outflow of the loch which can be seen flowing through a rocky channel below.

The outflow can only be crossed at low tide; even then it can be a tricky proposition. The water might still be knee deep and the channel is full of awkward, slippery seaweed-covered rocks and broken mussel shells, so you need to keep your boots on.

Once across*, carry on above the south side of the loch, following the marker posts westwards. Cross a drystane dyke and follow the marker posts above the shore of Loch Chromor and the stone-walled ruin of Dùn Cromore. Go through a gate by a house and follow the track road leading back into Cromore. Turn left at a T-junction to return to the main road with the phonebox to the left.

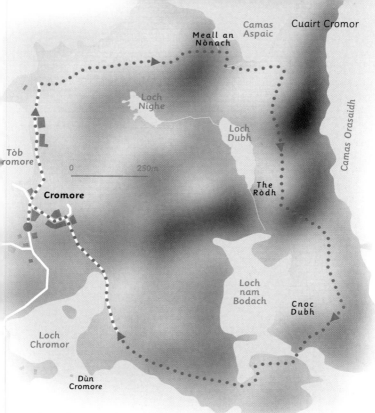

Cuairt Cromor

* If the outflow is too deep to cross, then head initially northwest around the shore of Loch nam Bodach. There are vague paths for much of the way. On the west side of the loch there are several old stock fences to cross. Rejoin the main path, picking up the marker posts by a drystane dyke at the isthmus between Loch nam Bodach and Loch Chromor. Bear right and follow the route as described in the paragraph above back to Cromore.

Index